Supporting mathematical development in the early years

2nd edition

Linda Pound

Open University Press

Open University Press
McGraw-Hill Education
McGraw-Hill House
Shoppenhangers Road
Maidenhead
Berkshire
England
SL6 2QL

email: enquiries@openup.co.uk
world wide web: www.openup.co.uk

and Two Penn Plaza, New York, NY 10121-2289, USA

First published 1999

A catalogue record of this book is available from the British Library.

ISBN–10: 0 335 21778 8 (pb) 0 335 21779 6 (hb)
ISBN–13: 978 0 335 21778 6 (pb) 978 0 335 21779 3 (hb)

Library of Congress Cataloging-in-Publication Data
CIP data applied for

Typeset by YHT Ltd, London
Printed in Poland by OZ Graf. S.A.
www.polskabook.pl.

Supporting mathematical development in the early years

Contents

Series editor's preface   vi

Introduction   1

1 Mathematics at home and at school   4

2 Successful learning: enjoying thinking mathematically   21

3 A curriculum to promote mathematical thinking   49

4 Implementing a curriculum for mathematical thinking   83

5 Observing, planning and supporting mathematical
   thinking and learning   118

6 Parents and professionals working together   140

Conclusion   151

References   154
Index   163

Series editors' preface

The publication of this second edition is testimony to the demand for and the success of a book of this kind. We believe that the first edition, in 1999, did much to help practitioners come to terms, not only with their own anxieties about mathematical understanding, but with how to help young children do the same. Since 1999, a major development has been the publication of the 'Curriculum Guidance for the Foundation Stage' (QCA 2001), the mathematical section of which has been much help to practitioners. The processes identified could quite easily have been based on the first edition of this book, in which Pound not only clarified the processes, but also showed the links between mathematics and other areas of the curriculum. They are, of course, still to be found in this second edition, and will continue to be of benefit to young children and their mentors.

This book is one of a series which will be of interest to all those who are concerned with the care and education of children from birth to 6 years old – childminders, teachers and other professionals in schools, those who work in playgroups, private and community nurseries and similar institutions; governors, providers and managers. We also speak to parents and carers, whose involvement is probably the most influential of all for chil-dren's learning and development.

Our focus is on improving the effectiveness of early education. Policy developments come and go, and difficult decisions are often forced on all those with responsibility for young children's well-being. We aim to help with these decisions by showing how developmental approaches to young children's education not only accord with our fundamental educational principles, but provide a positive and sound basis for learning.

Each book recognizes and demonstrates that children from birth to 6 years old have particular developmental learning needs, and that all those providing care and education for them would be wise to approach their work developmentally. This applies just as much to the acquisition of subject knowledge, skills and understanding, as to other educational goals such as social skills, attitudes and dispositions. In this series there are several volumes with a subject-based focus, and the main aim is to show how that can be introduced to young children within the framework of an integrated and developmentally appropriate curriculum, without losing its integrity as an area of knowledge in its own right. We also stress the importance of providing a learning environment which is carefully planned for children's own active learning. The present volume addresses the anxieties about mathematics, which still abound, in both adults and children, and offers us a variety of ways in which we can dispel them. The author shows us how quickly and how early on very young children start 'coming to terms' with mathematics, and how adults, both at home and elsewhere, can and should support and extend this early competence.

Access for all children is fundamental to the provision of educational opportunity. We are concerned to emphasize anti-discriminatory approaches throughout, as well as the importance of recognizing that meeting special educational needs must be an integral purpose of curriculum development and planning. We see the role of play in learning as a central one, and one which also relates to all-round emotional, social and physical development. Play, along with other forms of active learning, is normally a natural point of access to the curriculum for each child at his or her particular stage and level of understanding. It is therefore an essential force in making for equal opportunities in learning, intrinsic as it is to all areas of development. We believe that these two aspects, play and equal opportunities, are so important that we not only highlight them in each volume in this series, but also include separate volumes on them as well.

Throughout this series, we encourage readers to reflect on the education being offered to young children, through revisiting the developmental principles which most practitioners hold, and using them to analyse their observations of the children. In this way, readers can evaluate ideas about the most effective ways of educating young children, and develop strategies for approaching their practice in ways which exemplify their fundamental educational beliefs, and offer every child a more appropriate education.

The authors of each book in the series subscribe to the following set of principles for a developmental curriculum:

Principles for a developmental curriculum

- Each child is an individual and should be respected and treated as such.
- The early years are a period of development in their own right, and education of young children should be seen as a specialism with its own valid criteria of appropriate practice.
- The role of the educator of young children is to engage actively with what most concerns the child, and to support learning through these preoccupations.
- The educator has a responsibility to foster positive attitudes in children to both self and others, and to counter negative messages which children may have received.
- Each child's cultural and linguistic endowment is seen as the fundamental medium of learning.
- An anti-discriminatory approach is the basis of all respect-worthy education, and is essential as a criterion for a developmentally appropriate curriculum (DAC).
- All children should be offered equal opportunities to progress and develop, and should have equal access to good quality provision. The concepts of multiculturalism and anti-racism are intrinsic to this whole educational approach.
- Partnership with parents should be given priority as the most effective means of ensuring coherence and continuity in children's experiences, and in the curriculum offered to them.
- A democratic perspective permeates education of good quality and is the basis of transactions between people.

Vicky Hurst and Jenefer Joseph

Introduction

> We are, all of us, at all ages, already highly skilled
> mathematicians. We just haven't often learned it in our
> mathematics lessons.
>
> (Lewis 1996: 17)

There is widespread concern – from successive governments, from the
media, from the teaching profession itself – about standards of
achievement in mathematics. This concern is not new. In 1982, the
influential Cockcroft Report was published but even then, as the report
makes clear, anxiety about standards of mathematical achievement had
existed for well over a century before that. The Cockcroft Committee was
charged with reporting on mathematics in school and in the world of
employment. The report drew attention to the high number of apparently educated and intelligent adults who were unable to engage
comfortably in everyday activities because 'they are hopeless at arithmetic' (DES 1982: 5).

Over the ensuing twenty years throughout Britain, there have been
widespread curricular revisions, including the introduction of the
National Numeracy Strategy (NNS), which was designed to raise
achievement and improve the quality of learning and teaching in
mathematics. Despite the enormous range of curriculum changes, the
teaching and learning of mathematics remains the topic of much heated
debate in Britain. Even what we are talking about when we mention
mathematics is questioned. The term 'numeracy' is now frequently used

in place of 'mathematics'. But for many the use of the word 'numeracy' (like 'literacy') highlights the everyday uses, or functional aspects, of the subject. The NNS framework (DfEE 1999: 4) defines numeracy as 'a proficiency which involves confidence and competence with numbers and measures'. The document goes on to suggest that it involves:

- understanding of the number system
- computational skills
- inclination and ability to solve number problems in a variety of contexts
- practical understanding of the ways in which information is gathered . . . and presented.

Despite the apparent breadth of this definition, many – including many practitioners – feel that it underplays important aspects of mathematical thinking and development. While recognizing the important everyday or functional aspects of mathematics, some want to take a broader view of what mathematics is. Devlin (2000: 76), for example, writes that 'mathematics is not about number, but about life'. For him, study of mathematics involves consideration of pattern, cause and effect, the ability to think in the abstract and a range of other abilities.

The use of the term 'mathematical development' in the *Curriculum Guidance for the Foundation Stage* (QCA 2000) supports a focus on what children must learn and understand in order to develop as mathematical thinkers. It highlights the ongoing nature of mathematical learning and emphasizes the importance of approaching mathematics in ways which remain appropriate to the young child's developing understanding. This should not lead us to underestimate the competence with which young children learn to think mathematically. As Seo and Ginsburg (2004: 103) remind us:

> The bottom line is that preschool and kindergarten children's mathematics is more advanced and powerful than is often realized, and that children from different income-level groups display similar amounts, patterns, and complexities of mathematical behavior.

Neuroscience and developmental psychology underline the fact that humans are born mathematical (Pound 2004). Yet despite the fact that humans have a 'hard-wired' sense of mathematics and that mathematics permeates our everyday lives, a high proportion of the population remains convinced that mathematics is too hard for them. In a story about Barbie, Devlin (2000: 251) reminds us that 'maths is hard'. He tells of the manufacturer of Barbies having to drop the phrase 'maths is hard' from the dolls' repertoire of spoken phrases – since it was seen as undermining the attempts of educationalists to interest girls in mathematics. While supporting this view, Devlin reiterates his central thesis that it is hard, because it requires abstract thinking and precise reasoning. However, since humans are born mathematical (Pound 2004); and since we (and particularly young children) have 'puzzling minds' (Tizard and Hughes 1984) which enjoy challenge and stimulation, then mathematics ought not to be too hard for us!

This book sets out to show how competent young children are and how, if we wish to address low achievement, we should be building on all that children know and achieve in the early years. In this way we can support the achievement of individual children and, in time, of the British nation as a whole.

Chapter 1 gives an overview of young children's mathematical behaviour at home and in early years settings, contrasting that with the sometimes abrupt change that occurs on entry to statutory schooling.

In Chapter 2 the characteristics of learning in the early years which have a positive impact on all future learning are examined. In particular, the relationship between mathematics and language learning is considered. The way in which learning is most effective when based on children's 'persistent concerns' (Athey 1990), the role of representation in mathematical learning, mathematical connections (both neurological and in thought itself) and the need for children to develop a positive attitude towards mathematics are all examined. The importance of play and imagination to the development of abstract thought is considered.

Chapter 3 defines both the content and the learning curriculum (Claxton 1997) required to promote mathematical thinking. This will include some consideration of the use of Information and Communications Technology (ICT) to support mathematical thinking and development.

In Chapter 4, issues concerning the implementation of such a curriculum are considered.

The role of staff in observing, planning for and supporting children's learning by a variety of strategies is examined in Chapter 5.

The importance of a close partnership between the child's parents or principal carer and staff working in early years settings is explored in Chapter 6. Suggestions are made for promoting partnership.

Mathematics at home and at school

Mathematics is an important part of our everyday lives. The use of numbers for counting, ordering and quantifying measurements is recognized by all; asking for a specific number of items, turning left at the third set of traffic lights, buying a kilo of apples or half a litre of milk, deciding that even though the label says that a jacket is designed for a 6-month-old baby it will be too small for the baby we have in mind, estimating when to cook different dishes so that the whole meal is ready at the same time, and working out whether the cashier has given us the right change when we go shopping are all situations where we use mathematics with varying degrees of confidence. Becoming aware of the mathematics involved in, for example crossing the road, is salutary. In order to undertake this everyday task safely we have to:

- estimate the speed at which we can walk
- judge the speed of the cars coming towards us
- guess the distance to be travelled
- calculate how much time it will take us to cross from one side to the other.

How many times a day do we achieve this, without for one moment thinking about the mathematical computation which is going on in our heads?

Confusingly for children, we also use numbers as identifying labels – for example telephone, PIN and social security numbers. Notions of shape and space are part of our everyday mathematical understanding, too – working out how much carpet we need in square yards or square metres is one thing, but realizing that a long thin off-cut of carpet will be of less value to us than one which is closer to the squarish shape of the room, even though they are of a similar area, requires a different understanding.

But mathematics is much more than this – if our young children are to become confident and competent users of mathematics for the twenty-first century they will need to learn to recognize mathematics as a powerful tool for communication. Mathematics can help us to solve problems and to identify recurring patterns and themes. Most surprising of all, to some adults and children, is that it can be exciting, creative and enjoyable. Indeed, if it is to be of genuine use to young children growing up today, we must help them to revel in their mathematical thinking, to have confidence in their calculations and estimations and to develop a keen sense of curiosity about the ways in which mathematics touches and enhances our lives. They must develop not only mathematical knowledge, understanding and skills but also a disposition or inclination to enjoy learning and exploring mathematics. Above all adults must cherish and enhance the intensity, the ecstatic responses, the exuberance and joy which young children bring to their daily life, channelling it to support learning throughout their lives.

It is all too apparent that this is not the reality for most adults. The Cockcroft Report (DES 1982), referred to in the introduction to this book, demonstrated that, for many adults, mathematics is a subject to be feared. Many people acknowledged to the investigating team that they could not work out how much the petrol they needed would cost, could not add small sums of money and were often afraid of numbers. Ask any random group of adults to complete the sentence 'Mathematics is . . . .' and their responses are likely to include negative words such as *hard, complicated, difficult, painful, nightmare* or *boring.*

Many of the practitioners who work with young children share these negative attitudes. While we can sympathize we must also recognize that such attitudes can have a damaging effect on long-term achievement. Those of us who work with children have a responsibility to support the development of positive attitudes to mathematics alongside mathematical knowledge and skills – starting with ourselves!

In the following sections, the characteristics of children's mathematical development have been outlined. The stated ages are offered only as guidance – children's mathematical development, like so many other aspects of their learning, strongly reflects the culture within which they grow up. The characteristics outlined rest on three assumptions or tenets.

The first is that all learning (including mathematical learning) is shaped by the culture or context in which the child grows up. Children generally pay most attention to those aspects of a culture which they recognize as having particular significance for the people that are important to them in their day-to-day lives. Rogoff (2003: 262) writes that:

> Mathematical skills and tools are not all-purpose; rather they are adapted to the circumstances . . . When mathematics is used for practical purposes – such as by vendors, carpenters, farmers and dieters – people seldom come up with nonsense results in their calculations. However, calculations in the context of schooling regularly produce some absurd errors, with results that are impossible if the meaning of the problem being solved is considered.

The second is, as Clarke and Atkinson (1996: 25) remind us, that mathematical learning is not simply a question of learning things in a particular order:

> Children do not seem to learn maths in a linear way, learning one thing after another. It is a complex process. They often learn things that we don't think we have taught them, and fail to learn things that we think we have taught them. Learning seems to resemble a jigsaw, with concepts clicking into place as new experiences inform previous experiences.

Thirdly, the way in which parents and others caring for young children react to mathematics will influence the extent to which they feel able to behave as competent and confident mathematicians.

Mathematical thinking from 0 to 3 years of age

From birth, babies show remarkable abilities. Their inclination to work hard at making sense of the world around them means that within minutes of their arrival they are noticing events and forming hypotheses about cause and effect. In the early months of life, they are busy learning about mathematics as part of the explorations necessary for the process of becoming members of the community in which they live.

They learn about quantity – eagerly wanting an object, then wanting one for each hand, then realizing that they have no more hands and having to make decisions about which object to give up in favour of something new. In time, they will have to decide whether they would like two or three pieces of carrot and to understand that if sweets are on offer a different answer might be preferable. They will come to know what it means when told that they will have only two more songs before bedtime. This understanding will grow alongside the experiences which make the words a reality. Young babies are rarely taught to count in a systematic way but the concept grows as they listen to the tune of the language around them, hear the words and come to understand their significance. As the carer attempts to calm and dress the wriggling infant, his or her words 'one sock, two socks, one shoe, two shoes' will echo their playful sharing of 'one step, two step – tickling under there'. Counting the stairs as part of the bedtime ritual of a reluctant toddler is reinforced by and reinforces the singing of 'One, two, three, four, five/ Once I caught a fish alive . . .'

Babies of just a few days old have a surprising ability which is known as subitizing (Butterworth 2005). In some ways it ought not to be surprising because the ability exists in children and adults. It does however surprise us if we are used to thinking of babies not as the active learners that they are (Gopnik *et al.* 1999) but as passive blobs. Well-replicated research (Butterworth 1999, Dehaene 1997, Devlin 2000) indicates that in the first year of life babies can recognize a group of up to three objects, showing surprise when objects are added or taken away from the group. Karmiloff-Smith (1994: 173) comments on this ability, quoting from a mother's observation of her 5-month-old daughter:

> Sometimes we play games after she's finished eating in the high chair. She loves one where I take a few of her toys, hide them under the table top shouting 'all gone' and then making them pop up again just after. She squeals with delight. I once dropped one of the three toys we were playing with by mistake, and I could swear she looked a bit puzzled when I put only two toys back on her table.

Equally surprising is the notion that babies under 6 months can match two or three drumbeats to the same number of objects and that they register surprise when simple operations on groups of up to three objects (adding and subtracting Mickey Mouse toys) do not result in the correct number. Overall it appears from a wide range of studies that babies can:

- differentiate between cards with two or three dots
- differentiate between words with two or three syllables
- identify changes in the pattern of jumps made by a puppet
- recognize when shapes are added or taken away from a moving display of shapes on a computer screen
- demonstrate that numerosity (or the number of objects in a set) is

more important than the objects themselves by preferring to look at three toy buses when shown a picture of three teddy bears, than at the two teddies placed in front of them.

Recent research has questioned these findings and suggested that babies' interest in numerosity is linked not simply to an ability to subitize but also to brain maturation (Gifford 2005a citing Xu and Spelke 2000, and Xu 2003). Interest in babies' ability to track objects has led to research into their perception of larger numbers. While Gifford (2005a) suggests that babies' ability to discriminate between groups of objects can be confusing, Butterworth (2005: 6) reminds us that conflict between different brain systems is normal and leads to learning, as babies gain more experience of the world. He concludes that 'the current balance of evidence favours the idea that infants are able to represent the numerosity of sets of objects and carry out mental manipulations over these representations'. Gifford (2005a: 38) agrees that learning and maturation have an important role to play and writes that:

a complex picture emerges, whereby visualising, and symbolic representations of numbers develop interdependently suggesting that various areas of the brain work together to develop number understanding. Variations in experience, including language, counting practice and finger representations, seem likely to affect this development.

Babies are born with a propensity to seek out patterns and as we shall see this is an important aspect of mathematical development. Humans are good at recognizing faces, for example, and do it by looking for patterns. They learn more about time and pattern as the rhythm of their days unfolds, as carers move rhythmically and sing with them (Pound and Harrison 2003), and as the cycle of day and night becomes understood. (As many tired parents of babies who appear not to sleep at night can testify, some babies adjust to this pattern more readily than others.) The use of rhymes and songs plays a strong part in this growing understanding. Children as young as 5 or 6 months have considerable ability to predict timing and to maintain the rhythmic patterns found in traditional songs used with babies around the world (Trevarthen 1998). Moreover, they enjoy the humour as we deviate from the pattern – laughing with anticipation as the climax of 'tickling under there' or 'wee, wee, wee, all the way home' comes closer.

From their earliest days, straining to touch objects well beyond their reach or simply to grasp their own toes, babies are learning about distance. Their enormous efforts to move towards an object placed just out of their reach as they learn to crawl, grunting with frustration, show us the immense power of their drive to learn. As they start to move around on their feet, their first steps are supported as they estimate the distance between pieces of furniture, gauging whether or not they can get from chair to sofa without falling. Once upright, understanding of distance is further explored as toddlers use trucks and trikes, frequently crashing into doorways and scraping past the toes of others. With support and experience, toddlers can develop a good sense of distance.

Exploration of size and shape occurs when babies are given a variety of toys and household objects to play with. Selleck (1997: 15) gives a moving description of 7-month-old Samson's exploration of shape. She describes how he chooses to play with wheels – rolling a truck and twirling the dials on an activity centre. He watches older children playing on wheeled toys. Placed in his cot for a nap, he

> twizzles himself around the cot using his toes as levers and turns himself round like a wheel . . . using the power of his legs for spokes and his curling ratchet toes to grip the cot bars. Round and round, his eyes wide open, he takes in the dizzy, different perspectives of the kaleidoscope room . . . Samson is being a circle, a sensational embodiment of round and round . . .

The particular importance of Dorothy Selleck's observations of Samson is in giving status to what she terms 'Baby Art'. In relation to very young children's mathematical development, Samson's activity is most usefully viewed as an exploration and representation of his understanding of roundness. Art, like other modes of representation, is a tool for thinking (Matthews 2003; Davis 1997; Egan 1988) and as such supports and develops all thinking, including mathematical thought. At this stage of their lives, children's thought is primarily physical – described as 'enactive' by Bruner and 'sensorimotor' by Piaget. Toddlers' representations are rarely symbols made with markers but are more usually physical imitations of the concept being explored. If they have access to markers or paint, their representations will reflect the physical aspects of the object being represented. This is helpfully illustrated by Gardner's (1993: 75) description of a child in the early stages of developing symbolic representation who, when asked to draw a truck, will clutch the marker, hunch over the paper, and murmur, 'Vroom, vroom' as he passes the marker across the paper. Rather than creating a graphic equivalent of the truck, he instead converts the depicting moment into an enactment of the process of driving a truck along the road. In similar vein, Matthews (2003) describes his young son's paintings as 'a patterned dance in space and time'.

The chosen movements are likely to reflect the child's currently preferred style of physical action. In these early stages, this may be based on vertical lines, horizontal lines, or round and round scribbles (Athey 1990; Matthews 2003).

In emphasizing the importance of such 'ordinary and exceptional sensations', Dorothy Selleck advocates that babies are given the experiences that they need as the basis for their development as artists. The same sensations and experiences will, as Samson shows us, provide the material they will need to develop as thinkers and as mathematicians:

> All of us who care for and educate babies need to offer them the plural environments of toys in baby rooms and leafy mulchy gardens, meandering journeys, bustling markets, bubbling pools and all the places we visit and the people we meet . . . Babies need not be cloistered in warm plastic, swaddled in jingle music, or over protected in sterile fluffy, cuddly, cloying sweetness. A baby who is carried with us, maybe on our back with a wrapper, through household chores, out and about, will have the sensual experiences of the rhythms, sights, sounds and smells of their culture and communities to draw on . . .
>
> (Selleck 1997: 18)

Adults, both parents and carers, will support this early thinking and experience with language – providing labels and commentaries to enrich the ways in which very young children are beginning to understand the mathematical world around them. 'Up and down, up and down' accompanies the swinging movements that are part of adults' play with babies.

'Just one more button . . . and then you can get down' holds their attention as we finish dressing them. But some of the language comes from rhymes and songs, books and stories. These give young children a store of verbal ideas on which they can draw as their thinking develops. The words in isolation are often not fully comprehensible to the infant but within the context of interaction between adult and child they create sensations of belonging, communicating, anticipating, predicting and enjoying which will form the basis of all future learning.

Children's developing competence in using language also supports their growing ability to categorize (Gopnik et al. 1999). The oft-repeated 'What's that? What's that?' that usually occurs in the second year of life supports young children in acquiring a massive vocabulary of new words in a relatively short space of time. This 'naming explosion' is made manageable by the fact that children are simultaneously 'fast-mapping' (Gopnik et al. 1999: 115) or categorizing words in order to make them more memorable. That period where every man is 'dada' or every animal is 'cat' is part of the process of learning to categorize – an essential element of mathematical development.

Among the most important indicators of babies' mathematical ability is their drive to solve problems. From their earliest days, babies are driven to seek meaning, to puzzle things out (Tizard and Hughes 1984) to make sense of their world and to find ways to control it (Donaldson, 1992). In this they are no different from older humans (Gopnik *et al.* 1999).

Mathematical thinking from 3 to 5 years of age

The competence which babies and toddlers build up in their first three years of life continue to be developed throughout early childhood (and in some areas throughout life). The experiences on which their learning was based continue to be important, but over time some more explicitly mathematical experiences will be added. The ways in which the daily practices of the home affect children's learning have been well documented, particularly in relation to the development of literacy (for a summary see for example Worthington and Carruthers 2003). Just as parents who read a great deal, refer to programme schedules in order to find out what's on television, make shopping lists or order clothes from catalogues and menus from take-aways are supporting the development of literacy, so mathematical development is supported by explicit use of numbers and other aspects of mathematics in daily life. Using a calculator, referring to calendars, times and dates, and comparing weights or lengths supports children's development as mathematicians.

Conversely, there is evidence (Munn and Schaffer 1993) that children of this age do not naturally focus on number but will do so if the adults around them encourage them to do so. It appears, therefore, that young children's future ability to think mathematically, like other aspects of their development, depends heavily on the experiences, social interactions and accompanying language that children meet in these formative years. Copple (2004: 85) suggests that practitioners do not make sufficient use of this important aspect of development. She writes:

> Teachers or caregivers have closer contact with families (in the early years), and parents tend to feel more at home with them, than is the case with teachers in higher grades. However, the vast potential afforded by this rapport and daily communication is too rarely put to use by involving parents in promoting children's learning and

development, or even sharing with them much about what the child is learning and doing in the program, in mathematics, for instance. As for promoting children's enthusiastic encouragement with math, parents are almost never used as a resource.

At this stage in their development, children's attempts to represent their growing mathematical understanding may involve symbols, which will generally be based on a mixture of their own invented symbols and those that they have seen reflected in the culture around them. Some show at this early stage that they can differentiate between numbers and letters, even though they may not be sure which label to attach to them. If you watch young children busily filling in forms in banks and post offices, even quite young children often put letters in the writing spaces and numbers in the boxes intended for figures.

Research (Hughes 1986a; Worthington and Carruthers 2003) has highlighted the ability of young children to create symbols to help them remember numbers. Such work shows clearly that children can represent mathematical ideas in ways which they can remember if given meaningful situations. They can also represent zero – a concept which came relatively late to the field of human mathematical thinking. We as adults may not always find these invented symbols easy to interpret but this should not lead us to abandon attempts to encourage the use of such symbols but rather to seek to learn more and understand better (Worthington and Carruthers 2003)

Children's drawings at this stage of development show the beginnings of awareness of mathematical relationships, although sizes and quantities often reflect their personal and very subjective ideas. In drawing their families, for example, the size of each member of the group chosen by children of this age often demonstrates the pecking order identified by them, with themselves frequently larger than all others.

A spider drawn by John had many legs; although he knew that spiders have eight legs, his representation reflected the importance to him of the large number of legs which spiders have – the large quantity was for him more important than the specific number of legs.

Gradually these approximations give way to a more precise awareness of numerical quantities. Around the age of 4, children begin to want to count everything. Gardner (1993: 76) describes children at this stage of development as 'looking everywhere for evidence of numbers' counting the notes in a song, the buttons in their drawings of people and the letters on cornflake labels. David, approaching 4 years of age, while enjoying his bath, wanted to know how many bristles were on the nail brush. His mother replied that there were too many to count but if she really needed to know she could work it out by counting how many bristles there were in each cluster and by counting how many clusters of bristles there were. She further explained that she would then have to say that she had, for example, 36 lots of eight bristles. It was a fair assumption that this explanation had gone way over David's head – but no, over the next few days she was surprised to find him grouping his small cars, animals and blocks and saying, 'Oh look! I've got six lots of two. I've got three lots of three,' – delighted with the idea of clustering numbers.

Although interested in counting, young children are often still puzzling over the significance of numbers. Four-year-old Devon dictated a caption for his drawing, following the visit to the nursery of a police officer. The caption stated that 'the policeman had numbers on his shirt so anyone could phone him'.

Figure 1.1 When Victor (3 years) drew his family, he drew himself larger than his parents.

Counting demands a wide range of abilities, not all of which develop at the same time. Sometimes young children do not have ready knowledge of number names – a 3-year-old complaining to her nursery teacher about the unfair distribution of cars in the group where she was playing, held up three fingers and said 'Jane's got this many!'. Three-year-old Nick could correctly order number names and was aware that the last name given indicated the number in the group. However, in exclaiming to his dad, 'It's funny you know – I've got five fingers on this hand but ten on the other!' he demonstrated a gap in his understanding, namely that when counting you must always begin again at number 1. Sarah spent many happy hours wheeling her pram around the nursery gathering up all the dolls, teddy bears and fluffy animals she could find. She would then go out into the garden and spread them around on every available flat surface, before gathering them all up again. This behaviour went on over many days as Sarah explored the conservation of numbers.

Mummy   daddy   me

Figure 1.2 Julie (4 years 3 months) showed her good powers of observation and recognition of the relative sizes of things and people.

One-to-one correspondence is explored by children in a wide variety of ways – placing pretend cherries on pretend cakes, potato rings on fingertips, toy figures on top of piles of bricks and so on.

Similar explorations occur in relation to other aspects of mathematics. As children cram impossible amounts of clothes, dolls and dishes into bags and cases they are exploring quantity, area and weight, and, as they transport these from the role-play area to the book corner, distance. The pretend picnic which often forms an integral part of these games involves the child in unpacking and repacking, discovering what many of us find when we go on holiday – that apparently inanimate objects do appear to grow!

The work of Martin Hughes (1986a) has been very influential in alerting those who work with young children to their immense capacity for understanding and working with numbers. He underlines their abilities to carry out simple addition and subtraction using a range of strategies including their fingers. He shows that they can invent and recall their own systems of written number notation. They can learn to

Figure 1.3 Four-year-old Ben, who came to school by bus, wrote the bus number on the back of his bus.

make use of magnetic numbers and, over time, addition and subtraction symbols. They can use computer-driven robots. According to Hughes (1986a: 168):

> they do not confuse number with length, or fail to understand one-to-one correspondence, or believe that addition and subtraction do not alter numerosity. Rather, within their limits, they appear to be competent users of number.

He illustrates the limitations of young children's mathematical understanding, quoting the words of a number of 4-year-olds. The following conversations between Ram (aged 4 years 7 months) and Patrick (aged 4 years 1 month) and Martin Hughes are drawn from his research:

MH:	What is three and one more? How many is three and one more?
Ram:	Three and what? One what? Letter? I mean number?
MH:	How many is three and one more?
Ram:	One more what?

MH:	Just one more, you know?
Ram:	(disgruntled) I don't know.
MH:	How many is two elephants and one more?
Patrick:	Three.
MH:	How many is two giraffes and one more?
Patrick:	Three.
MH:	So how many is two and one more?
Patrick:	Six?

(Hughes 1986a: 45, 48)

What is clear is that if we offer children things to think about they can create images of unseen quantities. Patrick has no real elephants to count on a one-to-one basis – concrete thought depends not always on tangible materials but on ideas which make common or 'human' (Donaldson 1976) sense to children. Hughes (1986a) further suggests that young children's computational abilities are generally limited to small numbers. They do, however, enjoy large numbers and have some understanding of their relative values. Four-year-old Sean was playing with a calculator. He filled the digital display with strings of numbers, asking a student to read what he had written. He showed great enjoyment and persistence in being able to create 99 million. Gifford (1995: 105) writes of 3-year-olds, one of whom told his teacher that 'a million is more than a thousand' and the other of whom (Gifford 1995: 111), in looking at a calendar, successfully 'predicted the pattern 31 to 41 and 51, and [then] . . . wrote 55'. A girl watching wrote 505 (fifty-five), demonstrating some good though incomplete understanding.

Children's mathematical development does not progress in straight lines. It is often when children appear to have made a breakthrough in thinking that they suddenly revert to earlier understandings. This may be because they need the reassurance of more tangible, less abstract support for their thinking. In an incident described in *Wally's Stories* (Paley 1981), a group of pre-schoolers seek to measure two mats, dismissing the reliability of rulers and tape measures in favour of the length of classmates. Paley (1981: 14) writes:

> Wally announces a try-out for 'rug-measurers'. He adds one child at a time until both rugs are covered – four children end to end on one rug and three on the other. Everyone is satisfied, and the play continues . . .

However, the next day one of the rug-measurers is away and a major debate about age and size ensues, culminating with the teacher using a tape measure and showing them the number of inches each rug measures. To her surprise the children appear relieved when the absent child returns next day. She reminds them that they were able to measure the rug with the tape measure but, as Wally replies, 'Rulers aren't really real, are they?' (Paley 1981: 16). Knowing about standard measures does not guarantee that children believe in them!

In *Shoe and Meter* (Malaguzzi 1997) a similar situation is described. Although the children described are older (5 and 6 years of age) the issues explored throw up the same concerns for those involved in supporting young children's mathematical thinking. In a concluding section, Carla Rinaldi (1997) writes:

> The real problem, then, is not when and how to explain or present standard measuring instruments to children (at what age? in what way?), but rather to ask how we can create the conditions that enable the development of divergent and creative thought; how to sustain the ability and the pleasure involved in comparing ideas with others rather than simply confronting a single idea that is presumed to be 'true' or 'right' . . . All this is much truer and more important the younger the child is.
>
> (Malaguzzi 1997: 103)

Stories, books, songs and rhymes continue to play an important role in this exploration. Rehearsing number names in the right order requires a lot of practice which rhymes and songs allow in an effortless way. Books support children's exploration of reality and unreality in relation to mathematics in countless ways. Young children become engrossed in perennial favourites such as *The Very Hungry Caterpillar* (Carle 1969), *Rosie's Walk* (Hutchins 1968), *Six Dinner Sid* (Moore 2004) and *Handa's Surprise* (Browne 1995) as they explore quantity, size, position, time and probability. They rehearse the vital vocabulary necessary to describe quantities, patterns, shapes and amounts.

The play provision available in the group settings which most children of this age attend offers opportunities for exploring aspects of mathematics, but this is by no means more valuable than the child's home experiences. Worthington and Carruthers (2003: 183) suggest in fact that 'many young children come to school with a sense of mathematics which is never truly uncovered by their first teacher'. At home children take part in real tasks such as cooking, shopping, tidying and sorting, in situations where they can easily question what's happening. At its best, institutional care and education will complement all that the child has learnt and experienced at home, offering both real situations and opportunities to explore similar concepts in more abstract forms. Bead-threading cannot replace the patterns involved in setting the table – one is real and one is abstract. A water tray is not better than the bath, nor jigsaw puzzles necessarily more educational than packing shopping bags.

Mathematical thinking from 5 years of age

All the ways in which children have been learning about mathematics since birth – through physical action, play and exploration of materials and events, engagement in real-life experiences, discussion, questions and stories – continue to be important from age 5. However, entry to statutory schooling brings some changes. Howard Gardner (1993: 76) suggests that 'the universal decision to begin formal schooling around the age of five to seven is no accident'. By that age, he continues, children are comfortable with representing ideas and objects through a variety of media and they are beginning to demonstrate a 'readiness to use symbols or notations themselves to refer to other symbols'. This is a major developmental step but like other developmental steps depends upon the child's experience. Gardner (1993: 76) writes:

> Of course, the extent to which such notational behaviour is engaged in will reflect in part the prevalence of notational systems in a culture. Presumably children would invent marking systems much less frequently if they had not seen adults around them indulging in such activities. Thus does culture colour symbolization as clearly as it taints every other realm of early child development . . . the impulse to create a second-order symbol system – a set of marks that itself refers to a set of marks – is a deep human inclination that will emerge with relatively little provocation.

Sadly, as Gardner and many other writers show, despite this impulse it is precisely at this stage that many children lose their enthusiasm for mathematics. A range of writers, researchers and practitioners (see for example Clements and Sarama 2004) share the view that it is the failure to build on children's experiences before school, to work from the concrete to the abstract, to exploit children's interests, that limits later understanding. Carr (1992: 9) writes:

> A tentative assumption for early childhood practice might be that if the mismatch between common purposes at home and common purposes at the early childhood centre is too great, or if passivity is the expectation, children will retreat into purposes where others have the power: they may perceive that the purpose is to 'keep out of trouble', 'do as the adult expects', 'avoid anxiety', rather than to

take responsibility to influence the outcome, to seek a solution either to problems they have devised for themselves, or to help solve problems (as in supermarket shopping) which they know are meaningful for their community. The former option (where others have the control) provides opportunity to learn about other people and their attitudes; the latter (where children are able to take responsibility for the outcome) offers more potential for mathematical learning . . .

Those working with young children will be aware that children develop a firm understanding of mathematical (and other) concepts at different rates and in a different order. However, Gifford (1995) reminds us that the conventional reception class curriculum, with its emphasis on worksheets and colouring activities, frequently fails to tap into the knowledge and understanding that most young children already have. Their understanding of the language of measurement, position in space, selecting criteria for sorting, exploring, building and matching with shapes is often good. They show informal skills in number, such as counting, adding and subtracting, but are not usually able to represent their thinking in any formal way.

Our failure to build on what children know, albeit idiosyncratic and incomplete, often makes later learning more difficult. In later schooling the ability to 'count on' is painstakingly developed and fostered. Macnamara's (1996) research seems to indicate that it is precisely our failure to acknowledge young children's ability to recognize small groups of objects without counting them individually that contributes to the difficulty which many show in acquiring the later skill. She cites two interesting responses from school-age children. In one example, a boy who in the nursery had shown a good ability to recognize groups without counting, became distressed by being asked to do similar tests once he reached the reception class. On investigation he made it clear that it was not good enough to just say how many objects he could see – he insisted that he must count them 'saying that this was the way that they had to do it now they were in the reception class' (Macnamara 1996: 124). A further example indicates a link between 'counting on' and subitizing or recognizing groups without direct counting. Two 7-year-olds in the same study appeared to be able to recognize groups of nine or ten objects instantaneously. Asked to comment on how it was done, one said 'I always count some . . . I remember some and then I count the rest'. Macnamara (1996: 125) suggests that 'it seemed as if [he] could see some and label them with their size through subitising, and then (possibly) count on and add the rest'.

Summary

From birth children are learning about the things that humans have come to define as mathematics. To the young child they are not different from their other ways of coming to understand the world. They are learning too about the ways in which mathematics is used within their culture. They show remarkable ability to connect experiences gained from a variety of contexts in order to make increasing sense of what they have observed. An abrupt change occurs on entry to statutory schooling, when an emphasis is placed upon more formal and abstract ways of under-standing and representing mathematical thought. If children are frequently presented with tasks which are unconnected with their earlier ways of knowing about mathematics, they may come to reject it and to begin to feel that they are failing.

Successful learning: enjoying thinking mathematically

So few members of the general population have ever found fun or interest in mathematics, that the idea that it could possibly be enjoyable and involve playfulness and originality can be difficult to grasp. However, if the teaching and learning of mathematics are to become more effective and to have a positive, lifelong impact on children's lives, parents and early childhood educators will have to help children find in mathematics the play and creativity that is characteristic of their early development. Adults must learn to recognize and trust the mathematical learning that is occurring as the baby lurches between pieces of furniture, gauging the distances involved. The hours that young children will spend in lining up cars, putting dolls' clothes into sets, rolling and rerolling pastry scraps (which become progressively greyer) all contribute to their growing understanding.

In this chapter the ingredients of successful learning will be considered, beginning with the most successful learning that any of us ever achieve, namely spoken language. Mathematical development will then be considered in the light of other current views of learning.

Language, mathematics and representing mathematical ideas

The learning of our first language, which we do as babies, is central throughout our lives, free from anxiety and pleasurable. In contrast, many people think of their own mathematical learning as having been tedious, stressful and irrelevant to the mathematics which they use in their day-to-day lives. Those whose role it is to support young children's learning can make use of the huge body of knowledge about language as a way of understanding and promoting mathematical development.

It would be possible to dedicate many pages of this book to an argument about whether or not mathematics is a language, but whatever the outcome of such a discussion 'the *processes* associated with subjects like mathematics, science, art and music transform them into languages of learning' (Pound and Gura 1997). Table 2.1 compares the social and cultural factors which make language learning so successful in young children with the position which is frequently taken in supporting children's mathematical development.

Table 2.1 A comparison of the learning of language and mathematics in early childhood

Effective language learning as summarized by Harrison and Pound (1996: 236)	*Current approaches to mathematical learning and development*
1. Early efforts are strongly encouraged.	Our instinct with spoken language is to praise young children's every effort, whether grammatically correct or not. The lack of confidence felt by the majority of the population in mathematics is reflected in the fact that mathematical efforts are less acknowledged and understood. Adults are much more likely to insist on right answers and to discourage playing about with numbers.
2. Every utterance is treated as though it had communicative intent.	Adults take great pleasure in the fact that children are striving to communicate in spoken language. Even though adults regularly use mathematics in their everyday lives, very few are aware of the communicative potential of mathematics. It is not therefore surprising that they do not always identify and support it in children's utterances.
3. Learning is informal.	On entry to school, too often scant regard is paid to children's informal and home-based learning of mathematics. The use of schemes and worksheets all too easily discounts children's previous understanding and knowledge.

Table 2.1 (*continued*)

Effective language learning as summarized by Harrison and Pound (1996: 236)	Current approaches to mathematical learning and development
4. The rules of language use are learnt through talking and listening to others.	In our society in general there is insufficient discussion of mathematics for children to discern the rules. In societies and aspects of life where mathematics remains informal and largely unwritten, it may be more visible and explicit so that children can more clearly see how it is done, what it can do and how the rules work. Moreover, number words in some languages make the rules more obvious, such as those languages which use a form which broadly means ten-one rather than 11, ten-two for 12, etc.
5. Children hear adults all around them speaking fluently in a variety of ways and for a range of purposes.	Where adults do make their use of mathematics apparent and where they are confident in its use, children do well in mathematics when they enter school.
6. Children explore the possibilities of making vocal sounds.	Young children (and adults) play with language and its sounds a great deal (babbling, rhymes, nonsense words, jokes and so on); fewer opportunities for playing with mathematics are generally created at home or at school. Where adults lack confidence, they are less likely to see or exploit situations where play and exploration might happen. As Munn and Schaffer (1993: 76) comment 'very few adults regard numbers as objects of play'.
7. The emphasis is on communication rather than acquiring technical skill for its own sake.	Much mathematics teaching emphasizes abstract rules for 'doing sums'. Many children fail to see what the connection is between their ability to add or subtract numbers and real-life situations. Children's informal learning can be seen as both the starting point and as a stumbling block for later learning (Nunes 1996). Adults who work with young children as they enter school must ensure that they develop the former rather than the latter.
8. Children themselves set the pace and the sequence of their own learning, within a supportive structure provided by adults.	The view of mathematics as a jigsaw rather than a ladder of knowledge, skills, concepts and attitudes (Clarke and Atkinson 1996) is not always understood even by those who work with young children. The way in which

Table 2.1 (*continued*)

Effective language learning as summarized by Harrison and Pound (1996: 236)	*Current approaches to mathematical learning and development*
	many of those who work with young children were taught mathematics continues to affect the way in which we approach mathematics. Moreover, it continues to affect the views of parents, politicians and some policy makers!

Many primary school teachers find it difficult to approach mathematics in ways that have proved successful in children's development of their first language. They comment on their own lack of confidence, on the difficulty of working outside the school's scheme of work (whether commercial or home-grown) and on pressures from the National Curriculum (QCA 1999) from the National Numeracy Strategy (DfEE 1999) and from parents who were themselves 'taught by teachers that maths is rows of sums ticked in red' (Atkinson 1992: 10). It is not, of course, only parents who have a narrow view of what mathematics is. Atkinson's findings included the view that 'teachers are willing to try out new ideas but continue to believe that *real* maths comes out of a text book'. It is not at all surprising, then, that there are so many apocryphal stories of school-age children asking teachers who have been attempting to keep the curriculum relevant by focusing, for example, on mathematical games or discussion, 'When are we going to do our maths?'.

The playfulness that characterizes young children's language development (Trevarthen 1998) is rarely acknowledged in the learning of mathematics. Adults are less ready to regard children's apparent errors in mathematical terms as a joke than they are when the discrepancy occurs in language. This is a pity since 'playfulness, pretence and humour are particularly important for mathematics' (Gifford 2005a: 57). Three-year-old Luke, for example, attributed the large striped umbrella which was bounding along the beach on a windy day to an elephant which had picked up the umbrella with its trunk and thrown it up in the air. His family did not for one moment think that he was mistaken. They knew that he was playing with ideas and images. If, however, he had eaten four biscuits but claimed to have eaten two, or said that they were square when they were actually round, the family's reaction, and that of professionals, is likely to have been different. They would worry that he did not have a secure grasp of numbers or shapes.

The inventiveness with which young children use the linguistic resources at their disposal is well documented (Gopnik *et al.* 1999). Very young children use the few words they know to mean many things, including mathematical ideas. When a toddler says 'up' to mean 'I want to get up' or 'I want to get down' or 'Pick up my toy please' or 'Get the biscuit tin down please' we are delighted with their attempts to communicate and, when we can, comply with the request. Their creative use of mathematical language is not always readily understood. Kim, almost 2 years old, was nearly driven to a tantrum when she could not make her grandmother understand that when she said 'three' she meant 'a lot'. As her grandmother was tipping some raisins into a dish for her, Kim began to shout 'Three! Three!' Hearing (and responding to) the child's sense of urgency, the adult began to put some back into the packet. After several repetitions of this operation it was only when Kim's frustration drove her to try 'More three!' that she got her wish.

Using spoken language to represent ideas

Current models of teaching and learning in the early years emphasize the importance of sustained, shared conversations (Siraj-Blatchford et al. 2002; Durkin 2001), linking the role of communication to enhanced thinking (Goldschmied and Selleck 1996; Siegel 1999). This is in line with the approach promoted in the National Numeracy Strategy (DfEE 1999) and in the Curriculum Guidance for the Foundation Stage (QCA 2000).

It may however come as a surprise that not all writers and researchers wholeheartedly support this focus on spoken language. Tobin (2004: 123), for example, refers to the current emphasis on expressing ideas in words as 'logocentrism'. He highlights the importance of sensorimotor thinking and feeling and suggests that insisting on the expression of ideas verbally may suppress important ways of knowing and under-standing. Phillips (1998: 40), writing from a psychoanalytical perspective echoes this view. He writes that 'there are areas of experience, realms of feeling that seem resistant to speech'.

These are of course extreme points of view but they should act as a reminder that an emphasis on spoken language should not cut across young children's intuitive, physical and sensory ways of thinking. What seems vital, as Claxton (1997) himself acknowledges, is that putting ideas into words must not *supplant* but *supplement* other forms of representation. The work of early educators in Reggio Emilia offers a model for thinking about a range of representational forms or ways of knowing, called the 'hundred languages of children'. Practitioners encourage children to make a range of representations, perhaps of the same object over time, in a variety of materials, from different perspectives and through the use of senses in unconventional ways such as drawing sounds and representing objects through sound and movement. In their view, oral language is seen as one of many possible representational forms.

The work of Mithen (1996) offers further support for emphasizing the role of oral language. He suggests that it is spoken language which from our earliest days gives us the ability to move between different ways of knowing – to shift between thinking intuitively and thinking logically; to connect ideas learnt at a parent's knee to those learnt in other situations. Early humans could communicate, make tools and interpret information about their natural worlds such as recognizing hoof prints. Mithen suggests that these skills were compartmentalized within specific areas of the brain. Only as we developed language did we become able to transfer knowledge and understanding from one area of expertise to another. Language made humans more aware of their abilities.

Around the world, non-literate societies use story, song and rhyme to help them think (Egan 1988). Since little children are almost by definition non-literate, the importance of these verbal ways of knowing should not be overlooked. Talking, discussing, explaining, singing, chanting and reciting play a part in establishing children's knowledge and under-standing. In addition, story, song and rhyme contain two further elements which make them vital in young children's development. All provide an opportunity to explore rhythm and narrative through physical movement. Rhythm promotes dance while drama encourages physical play (Duffy 1998).

Representing and translating mathematical ideas

The work of Piaget, Bruner (1986) and Gardner (1993) has a common theme – long before children are able to think in abstract terms they will have represented their ideas in physical action (enactive or sensorimotor thinking). This form of representation can begin within hours of birth, when tiny infants struggle to mimic the facial expressions of their mother (Trevarthen 1998). Publicity materials from Reggio Emilia include a wonderful photograph of a baby in arms looking at a large shell and spreading her fingers to represent its shape.

At a later stage, their theories suggest, children will supplement these early actions by representing objects, events and ideas with a selection of materials. They will choose and organize (or sometimes literally stumble across) objects and materials to stand for other things (iconic thinking). Two-year-old Graham, for example, found a twig in the garden and rushed in to show his mother how it matched the illustration of the wolf in a favourite story of the moment, *The Three Little Pigs* (Stobbs 1968).

Emma, at 16 months old, spent long periods sorting her toys, house-

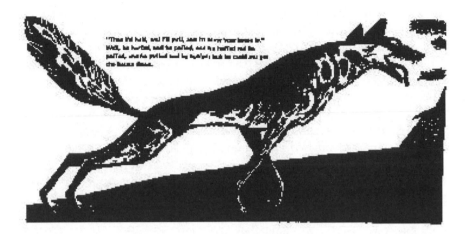

Figure 2.1 The wolf in 'The Three Little Pigs', represented by a twig by 2-year-old Graham.

hold objects and sticks and leaves. She tore one red and one white paper napkin into tiny pieces and then became completely absorbed in sorting the shreds into piles of red or white scraps. Max, at almost 2 years of age, begins to apply this sorting activity to comparing representations, demonstrating an understanding of the link between different representational forms:

> Max has started comparing objects. If he sees a penguin on TV then he goes to his box of animals and picks out a penguin. He'll do the same with pictures. He also moves objects around and will line all his animals up on the settee and then move them all somewhere else.
>
> (Karmiloff-Smith 1994: 195)

Gradually, children find a variety of ways of representing things symbolically – through sounds (musical and verbal), colours, models, images, movement, stories and imaginative play. Written forms of symbolic representation require high levels of abstraction and are based on these earlier more physical representations.

The thinking processes adopted by young children are not the same as those adopted by adults. Through experience, development occurs which over time produces qualitative changes in the way in which children think (Bruner and Haste 1987; Gardner 1993). Bruner's idea that we all fall back on earlier stages of symbolization when confronting new or difficult ideas makes common or (to use Donaldson's term) 'human sense'. We have all, at some point when computation has let us down, reverted to moving little piles of money around in order to get our sums right.

These theories about thinking and representation are largely based on the work of Piaget, who is not without his critics. Almost 30 years ago, the seminal book *Children's Minds* by Margaret Donaldson (1976) underlined the strengths but also pointed out the limitations of his work. The strengths include the respect that his work generated for young children's minds and the way in which he opened people's eyes to the idea that young children have reasons for what they say and do.

Recent studies underline the inappropriate expectations which Piaget's work may have established in the minds of practitioners. Merttens (1996) criticizes Piaget's work as imposing a glass ceiling on children's ability to learn and understand. She suggests that the emphasis which has been given to *stages* of development has promoted an underestimation of children's ability. Far from being the 'primitive thinkers' which Piaget's work may have led us to believe they are (Merttens 1996), young children have shown themselves capable of extraordinary powers of abstraction. She describes 5-year-olds imagining small numbers of objects and being able to perform number operations on them in their heads. These high expectations are qualified by her statement that 'children will only feel confident at this mental activity when they have actually played similar hiding games'. This view is in line with the work of Hughes (1986a) who has consistently demonstrated that, given appropriate conditions (such as the use of relatively small numbers) children are able to work effectively with abstract concepts.

Piaget's work focusing on children's logic is compelling and has led many to respect children's thinking. However, these ideas also highlighted the role of logic in thought and in particular in mathematical thinking. Gardner (1999: 42) has been critical of the way in which logic came to be more highly valued than other kinds of thinking. Gardner writes that 'Piaget claimed that he was studying all of intelligence, but I believe he was actually focusing on logical-mathematical intelligence.' For Gardner mathematical thinking requires much more than logical-mathematical intelligence. This view is shared by Devlin (2000) who identifies logic as just one of many processes required to think mathematically. He suggests (as outlined in Chapter 1) that a range of processes including hypothesizing (or guessing), identifying pattern, categorizing and linking cause and effect support mathematical thinking. In particular he suggests that imagination is a vital component in learning to think in the abstract ways required for mathematics.

Claxton (1997) recognizes the qualitative shift which occurs in children's thinking and alludes to the ever-growing range of experiences which young children face as they visit more places, enter nursery, meet new people and encounter new ideas. Claxton reminds us that we would all benefit from making use of intuition, imagination, observation, phy-sical action, feelings and dreams. He stresses that these ways of developing learning and understanding should not be got out of the way as quickly as possible, as politicians seem to wish us to do. On the contrary they should form the bedrock of future learning, and not be overshadowed by more formal approaches. Because such approaches are found in children, we should not assume that they are childish.

Using and translating a variety of symbolic languages

Young children will understand and use conventional symbol systems more effectively when they know how these connect with their own ways of representing things. The Froebel Blockplay Research Group (Gura 1992: 90) gives an example of a child's invented symbolic repre-sentation being used, with the help of his nursery teacher, to help him think mathematically. Edward's teacher has reminded him that he will have to clear away the blocks in five minutes.

(Edward appears to ignore this and carries on selecting blocks. Seconds later, he appears in front of his teacher.)

Edward: How many minutes was that? Five? (He has five narrow cylinders gathered to his chest.) These are your minutes, right? (He places them in a line, counting as he puts each one down.) One, two, three, four, five.

Teacher: D'you want me to take one away every time a minute is used up?

Edward: Yes. Let me see your watch. (The teacher indicates the minute hand. Together they watch the passing of one minute. As the hand sweeps past the twelve, Edward jumps and punches the air with a fist. Yeah! he shouts, before laying flat one of his cylinders.) 1–2–3–4 minutes to go, everyone! (He counts his remaining 'minutes' and continues marking time in this way, subtracting a block for each minute as it passes and counting the remainder, until all the cylinders are flat. He becomes so absorbed with his tally he completely forgets the object of the exercise.)

Interestingly, Hughes (1986a) has used the term 'translation' to describe the process of moving between different representations of mathematical ideas. This is the same term as that used in Reggio Emilia in considering the hundred languages of children. If children are to be successful in thinking about mathematics, Thumpston (1994: 114, citing Hughes 1986a) suggests that:

> The concept of 'translation' provides an important way of thinking about mathematical understanding. The ability to translate fluently between different modes of representation is of paramount importance, yet it is the source of many difficulties which children have with mathematical problems . . . Children need help to form links between formal and concrete understanding, building on their informal methods of calculation and their invented symbolism in order to develop, understand and use more powerful formal modes of representation.

The more powerful formal modes of representation to which she refers are second-order symbolizations, such as writing and numbers. These symbols representing symbols must be based on a firm foundation of children's own invented symbols. Egan (1988: 212) emphasizes the importance of encouraging children to see the connections between the ways in which they represent their own ideas and the ways in which other people choose to do so. He writes that 'while we are encouraging children to be makers and shapers of sounds and meanings we will also give them many examples of other people's shapes'. It is the process of translating between these representations that helps children to understand the world.

A reception class teacher helped children in her class to translate between different symbolic languages by simple but effective means. She put up an eye-catching display about their trip to the park. A significant part of the display was taken up with a variety of representations of the children who had been on the visit. Play People reflecting the numbers of boys, girls and adults who had gone were supplemented by drawings, tallies and graphs (created by teacher and children in a variety of forms), written and photographic representations. Children enjoyed counting and recounting the objects and studying the representations.

Tracking Leroy during his day at nursery school revealed that he had spent time at the graphics table drawing himself and liberally sprinkling the paper with fours. He had put four straws into each of the sand pies he had made in the sand pit and four balls of dough to represent cherries on each of his dough cakes at the dough table. He had found four little speckled frogs in a book made by the teacher in the book area and all the cards depicting sets of four from a number game. It came as no surprise that he had just had his fourth birthday.

In most children's development, the steps associated with translating between different forms of representation can be rapid and almost imperceptible. For children with learning difficulties, gradual steps may need to be identified by adults to help them to understand how one thing can stand for another. From knowing that a drink is available only when they actually taste it, children with learning difficulties can be helped to understand that it is drink time when shown a cup or, by gradual stages, half a cup, a cup handle, a picture of a cup, the sign for a cup and the word for a cup. When we witness this painstaking process we are reminded of the wonderful achievement of translating and coming to understand the variety of representations that is virtually hidden in most children's development.

There is a danger that current requirements on those working with 4-, 5- and 6-year-olds to meet the demands of the early learning goals in the Foundation Stage, the National Curriculum (QCA 1999) and National Numeracy Strategy (DfEE 1999) will undermine young children's drive to represent experiences and ideas in a variety of ways and through a range of media, in ways which have special meaning for them. This is particularly sad when we realize that the emphasis on some of the more formal aspects of literacy and numeracy which has resulted from downward pressures has more to do with adults' perception of what is meant by the documents than with what is actually written (Edgington *et al.* 1998). The early learning goals do not *require* children under 5 to be able to record number operations formally. Pressures to accelerate children into the use of conventional notations and symbol systems may, in the short term, result in apparently rapid progress in, for example, doing simple sums but will not lead to high later achievement.

Apparently 'slower ways of knowing' (Claxton 1997) are not always slower in the long run, as Merttens's (1996: 31) comment that 'accumulated evidence from the last century show[s] unequivocally that too early an introduction to formal arithmetic hinders children's numeracy' reminds us. Thumpston (1994: 121) also reiterates the importance of taking a long-term view of children's learning:

Schools can train children to become skilful operators, to perform well in the short term but this does not develop the network of connections, symbolic representations and meanings which extends the power of thinking and hypothesising.

Mathematical learning and the brain

New technologies including a range of brain imaging techniques (see for example Karmiloff and Karmiloff-Smith 2001) have given us access to a whole range of new insights into the process of learning. Bill Lucas (2001) has produced a readable and general account of recent developments in understanding and suggests that the brain operates at its best under the following circumstances:

- The brain thrives on patterns.
- The brain loves to explore and make sense of the world.
- The brain likes to make connections.
- The brain loves to imitate.
- The brain does not perform well under too much stress.

(based on Lucas 2001: 18-21)

Table 2.2 The links between aspects of learning and mathematical development

Aspects of learning (based on Lucas 2001: 18–21)	Aspects of mathematical development
The brain thrives on patterns	Mathematics has been called 'the science of patterns' (Devlin 2000). The human brain is good at identifying patterns. The process begins at birth as babies are drawn to the pattern of human faces (Murray and Andrews 2000). By 6 months of age babies can identify faces (including the faces of monkeys) more efficiently than adults. This ability is what has enabled the human brain to develop mathematical thinking and should be exploited in enabling young children to make sense of mathematics in the classroom.
The brain loves to explore and make sense of the world	Since mathematics is about life (Devlin 2000), it provides a way of making sense of the world. This process is supported through language and exploration but it also thrives on narrative, *play and imagination*. These enable children to explore the world including mathematical ideas.
The brain likes to make connections	Learning really only occurs when connections are made between things that are known and new information and experience. In order to support mathematical development we should find ways to enable children to *make connections* between what they already know and what they are learning. Human imagination also allows us to make connections between things that are real and things that are not real.

Table 2.2 (*continued*)

Aspects of learning (based on Lucas 2001: 18–21)	Aspects of mathematical development
The brain loves to imitate	Imitation is sometimes thought of as a simple process but as Donaldson (1992) reminds us it is far from that. This aspect of learning relates to the *cultural* aspects of mathematical development which were referred to in Chapter 1. It also however refers to the *social* aspects of mathematical learning. Children benefit from sharing mathematical ideas with adults and with their peers. This of course makes the opportunity to discuss mathematical ideas (as explored earlier in this chapter) crucial to effective mathematical learning.
The brain does not perform well under too much stress	Fun and *positive dispositions* are of paramount importance in sound mathematical development. Many of the adults who find maths so difficult were probably taught in ways which made the subject a painful experience. Young children need to enjoy mathematical experiences if they are to become excited by the subject.

Play and imagination

Until recent years, play and imagination were generally thought of as contributing to mathematical development simply by offering first-hand experience from which children developed the concepts which support future mathematical learning. The more recent insights of neuroscience have underlined and strengthened this view. As Susan Greenfield (1996: 75) tells us: 'Play is fun with serious consequences.' The rich experiences which arise in imaginative play contribute to learning in general by creating millions of connections in the brain. In addition, they contribute to mathematical development by supporting children's ability to think in the abstract.

Mazur (2003) has written with great passion about the relationship between imagination in the arts and mathematical imagination. His focus is higher mathematics (or what some people call 'hard sums') but he succeeds in demonstrating something of the play and creativity involved in mathematical thinking. Devlin (2000) writes more specifically about the way in which abstract thought can be seen as developing through four distinct stages.

Table 2.3 Stages of abstract thought (based on Devlin 2000: 118)

Level of abstract thought	Description (based on Devlin 2000: 118)	Examples	Implications for young children's learning
1	Thinking about real objects in the immediate environment, but may be imagined in different locations, or arranged in different ways	Devlin suggests that many animals seem capable of this level of abstract thought, although he adds that there is 'really no abstraction at all'. For him it serves as a sort of baseline for thinking about the process of abstraction.	Rich first-hand experiences feed this level of thought. The extended childhood of humans enables them to build rich foundations for thinking.
2	Thinking about real familiar objects which cannot be perceived (seen, heard, smelt or felt) in the immediate environment	Devlin suggests that monkeys and apes may operate at this level.	This level of thinking may be supported by encouraging children to make connections between things in the environment and things they know about but which are not apparent. They might for example be encouraged to say what a particular sound or smell reminds them of. Questions such as 'What does this shape make you think of?' can promote this level of thinking.
3	Thinking about real objects that the individual may never have seen, or imagined variations/combinations of real objects. Language users operate at this level of abstraction	Unicorns are a good example of abstract thought at this level. They combine two things which humans have encountered (animals with horns and horses). From these an unreal animal has been imagined.	At this level play and imagination contribute much to abstract thought. Representational forms including stories, painting, dance, exploration with sounds, blocks and other construction materials, imaginative

Table 2.3 (*continued*)

Level of abstract thought	Description (based on Devlin 2000: 118)	Examples	Implications for young children's learning
			play and other representational forms all contribute.
4	Mathematical abstract thinking which need have no link with anything in the real world	2 + 2 = 4 need not relate to anything at all. It can be thought about in an entirely abstract way.	The conversation described in Chapter 1 between Patrick, Ram and Martin Hughes is an excellent example of young children developing this level of abstract thinking. In the early years a range of activities can be used to help children to visualize in ways which help them to make sense of abstract mathematical ideas. These will be explored further in Chapter 4.

Persistent concerns

Whenever or wherever we observe young children, what Athey (1990) has called their *persistent concerns* readily become apparent. Whether they are interested in trains or worms, or in the three Fs which Paley (1988) identifies as the overwhelming concerns of young children – namely fairness, fantasy and friendship – their current passions make themselves felt in a variety of ways. Persistent concerns are an effective starting point for the education of young children. For babies they are the *only* effective starting point. It is very difficult indeed to get them to shift their focus of attention from preferred objects. When babies become interested in a particular object, person or event, they effectively block out other sources of stimulation. Try as adults may to distract their attention, they continue to stare at whatever they are interested in, sometimes performing impossibly athletic movements in order to keep it in view.

As children become older and more experienced it gradually becomes more possible to attract their attention, but their enthusiasms remain important. We should not regard them as a barrier to what we want children to learn but should regard their interests as part of their task of learning how to learn. As their social awareness grows they become susceptible to the concerns and interests of the group and it is at this stage that group topics and projects (informal as well as more structured ones) hold sway in children's learning. Menmuir and Adams (1997: 34) remind us of the advantage that adults gain when they work with children's persistent concerns:

> The starting point is a challenge and a challenge is anything that confronts the learners with the need to begin asking their own questions . . . it is better to start from children's 'persistent concerns' and link these to intentions for learning supplied by the adult.

Depending on their age and stage of development, children will talk about their consuming interests, draw pictures, make models, act out relevant situations from a mixture of their experience and their imagination, play with objects which represent their current enthusiasm and seek out photographs, paintings, songs, rhymes and models associated with it. Three-year-old Oliver was fascinated by Robin Hood. The books and videos, the hat with the feather and the bow and arrows were vital components of every day. Each morning he would awake with another idea for developing and modifying his bow and arrows.

These concerns sometimes have direct and easily recognizable mathematical connections. As discussed in Chapter 1, Gardner (1993) reminds us that, at about 4 years of age, many children have a consuming interest in counting. Seymour Papert developed Logo, a computer program which even young children can use effectively to make things happen – either on the computer screen or, when connected to a small vehicle known as a turtle, with movements on the ground. Papert (1982) describes his passion for the mathematics of cogs and ratios which emerged in early childhood after visiting a mill.

Sometimes, while not solely connected to mathematics, the current concern links with something which incidentally engages the child in mathematical ideas and activities. Three-year-old Christopher, for example, was obsessed with buses. He collected pictures of buses and knew every book in the book corner which had so much as a hint of a bus in it. His drawings led to numerous discussions about bus numbers. If he was drawing a number 6 bus he wanted to be sure that people were going to get on the right one! His dramatic play included a wide range of mathematical ideas – tickets, money, numbers and the arrangement of seats are just some of the possibilities which he explored in his play.

Table 2.4 Children's persistent concerns as demonstrated in schema and their relevance to mathematical development (based on City of Westminster nd; Manning-Morton and Thorp, 2001 Section 8: 9)

Schema	Definition	Examples	Relevance to mathematical development
Assembling	Bringing things together in random piles or more structured arrangements	Piling toys onto an adult's lap	Exploring quantity and estimation – the different ways in which objects are grouped can make them look very different.
Transporting	Moving objects or collections of any kind from one area to another	Using a bag, truck, crane to carry all the bricks, sand or dishes from one place to another; pushing a friend in a toy pram	Exploring conservation of quantity – if I move these things are they still the same things, is there still the same amount?
Positioning	Placing objects in a particular position	Lining up cars; sitting dolls in rows; organizing queues; walking round the edge of the sandpit; lining up toys round the edge of the table	Categorizing Sequencing Comparing Creating patterns Exploring shape and size
Orientation	Interest in a different viewpoint	Hanging upside down; turning objects around and upside down; peering backwards with head between legs	Quite literally getting a new perspective on the world. If I see something upside down is it the same, is it different, how does it change?
Dab	Random or systematic marks forming patterns or representing objects	In painting and drawing representing eyes, flowers, buttons, snow or rain etc.	Filling space Exploring area Exploring quantity

Table 2.4 (*continued*)

Schema	Definition	Examples	Relevance to mathematical development
Trajectory, diagonality, horizontality, verticality	Exploration of horizontal and vertical lines, separately and then in combination to form crosses or grids; interest in diagonal lines, zigzags	Lines in paintings, construction, block building, climbing, throwing – swords, planes, net; ramps, slides, sloping walls, roofs, saws, serrated knives, sharks' teeth; dropping things from the cot, interest in running water from taps, hoses; throwing, climbing and jumping	Exploring space and shape, size and distance
Enclosure/ containing	Forerunner of area – enclosure left empty or carefully filled in	Fences, barricades with blocks or Lego; enclosing painting, drawing or writing within a line; filling and emptying containers; sitting in tunnels or large boxes; building cages, houses, garages etc. with blocks	Exploring area and size – how big an enclosure does this shape, quantity etc. require?
Enveloping/ wrapping	Completely covering objects, space, themselves; wrapping things up	Putting things in bags, pockets, parcels; painting over picture; covering with blanket or flannel; cuddling	Exploring quantity, size, shape – how much string/ paper, sticky tape do I need to cover this box, wrap up this parcel? Problem-solving

Table 2.4 (*continued*)

Schema	Definition	Examples	Relevance to mathematical development
Circularity and semi-circularity	Exploring curved lines; awareness of circles then half circles	Heads, bodies, eyes, wheels, thread, rope, string	Exploring size, shape, distance, quantity
Radial	Lines radiating out from a core	Spiders, sun, fingers, hair	Exploring space; identifying patterns, similarities and differences
Rotation	Exploring things that turn	Wheels, cogs, rolling cylinders, observing and/or constructing rotating parts e.g. washing machines, windmills; enjoying spinning round or being swung round	Problem-solving Exploring space, shape
Connection/ separation	Fastening or joining things together; taking things apart	Train track and carriages; tying knots; staples, paper clips, masking tape; linking various objects; drawings with linked parts; children's 'maps'	Exploring connectedness – a vital aspect of all learning including mathematics
Ordering	Putting things in order	Size – largest, smallest; number; pattern in beads, pegs, drawings, songs	Aspects of ordering, sequencing, categorizing etc.
Transforming	Interest in change in materials/life	Mixing paint etc.; cooking; ice melting; clay hardening; eggs hatching; seeds	Transformation is a vital aspect of all learning including mathematics. The idea that numbers,

Table 2.4 (*continued*)

Schema	Definition	Examples	Relevance to mathematical development
		growing; tadpoles developing; butterflies hatching; adding juice to mashed potato, sand to the water tray	shapes, measures etc. can be changed by particular operations is important to future understanding.
Perforation	Making holes	Cutting, nailing, sewing	Like dabs, supports the exploration of quantity, space and area
Correspondence	Matching things together 1-1	Cup and saucer, knife and fork, nappy for each doll	1-1 correspondence important to early counting; paves the way for thinking about 1-4 (e.g. sharing a cake) or 3-1 (e.g. three candles on one cake)
One, two etc.	Patterns of a particular number	4 panes in each window, 5 petals in each flower	Identifying and creating patterns; counting; learning to understand the abstract notion of 'fourness' – that it can apply to all sorts of things

Athey (1990) found that children's representations of their experiences (whether in play, modelling or drawing) reflected their current spatial interest or *schema* (see Table 2.4). Nutbrown (1999) discusses children with a dominating interest in *schema*, which may lead to their involvement in activities and ideas concerned with such mathematical ideas as height (dynamic vertical schema), rotation (dynamic circular schema) and capacity (containing/enveloping schemas). Whalley (1994: 96) describes 3-year-old Jacob who attended Pen Green Nursery Centre where staff plan and support children's learning through their observations of children's interests and schema. Jacob

> has, according to his parents, shown an interest in string since the age of twelve months. The nursery provision includes lots of balls of string which Jacob finds fascinating. He persists in unravelling and ravelling the string and winding it between chairs and furniture and outside among the trees. He is particularly interested in length; how far will the string stretch? He enjoys cutting different lengths of string and ties it to door handles. He is very concerned that the string must not touch the ground and is distressed when other children follow his string-tail and walk on it.

Whether these interests are enduring or short-lived, they provide the motivation for children's exploration and learning. They enable them to become experts and the knowledge of what it means to be a specialist can support the development of expertise in other areas. Pound and Gura (1997: 25, citing the work of Inagaki 1992) refer to a study

> involving young children who were given a goldfish each to look after for several weeks. Not only did they become experts on goldfish . . . they were also able to use this knowledge and know-how to speculate about other forms of life and as a springboard to other kinds of knowledge and skill.

Being an expert gives children familiar material with which to play and which they can think about. Expertise, moreover, gives children the opportunity to create their own analogies and to translate the ideas with which they are presented in a way which makes sense to them.

Practitioners who work with children who have autistic spectrum disorders are extremely familiar with what in such children are regarded as obsessive behaviour. Opinions vary as to the extent to which autistic children should be encouraged or discouraged from enacting or talking about the topics with which they are currently obsessed. The Public Autism Awareness website (www.paains.org.uk/cats/interventions. htm) identifies strategies for dealing with obsessions but states that where appropriate special interests may be used to support other learning. Manning Morton and Thorp (2001 section 8: 8) suggest that 'children with special educational needs have schemas but they may need additional help in applying them to a wide range of situations'. The fact that such special interests are associated with autistic spectrum disorders should not deter teachers and other practitioners from recognizing the value of working with most children's passions. When following up their enthusiasms most children are simply learning to learn with enthusiasm. Practitioners need to decide how to harness the aspects which can be seen to serve long-term development.

Making connections

> We have heard much about the poetry of mathematics, but very little of it has yet been sung.
>
> (Henry David Thoreau)

> Pure mathematics is, in its way, the poetry of logical ideas.
>
> (Albert Einstein)

Mathematical learning, like all other, depends upon making connections – connections which are both physiological (apparent in the brain itself) and psychological (the ideas which pop into our minds, sometimes apparently unbidden). The logic and the poetry of mathematics are rarely connected in our classrooms, yet it is precisely surprising connections of this sort which help children to learn to think creatively. The playfulness which is characteristic of creative thought is essential to human development (Mithen 2005). Those who were the pioneers of the early childhood tradition in Britain understood that time and space were essential ingredients for children, learning through their play with materials and ideas (McMillan 1930). Their view is reiterated by Claxton (1997) who underlines the importance of taking time to create playful links, not just in early childhood but throughout life.

Children's ability to make these sorts of links needs to be fostered early in their development since this is when neural connections are being established in the brain. There is increasing evidence that if children are to realize their full potential mathematically, as well as in other areas of experience, we must ensure that they make good use of both sides of the brain. This will ensure the development of the physical and neurological links which will help them to become good problem-solvers and mathematical thinkers. Within our culture, a heavy emphasis is placed on the logical, rational, factual and analytical approaches to learning (Atkinson and Claxton 2000) which are generally supported by the dominant hemisphere of the brain. (For most people this is the left side.) The non-dominant hemisphere guides aspects of our understanding such as spatial awareness, emotion, intuition, making connections, ability to respond to music and to react to colour (Odam 1995; Ramachandran 2004). If we want children to develop both logical and poetic mathematical abilities we should from a very early stage be supporting thought in both areas of the brain. Of particular importance to early childhood educators is Odam's (1995: 13) claim that 'movement learning is the oldest and most basic learning we experience and it can enhance and modify the effectiveness of both right- and left-brain learning'. It is physical movement which enables humans to develop complex thinking in both halves of the brain. As such it is vital to the education of young children.

Connecting formal and informal mathematical knowledge and understanding

Many of the difficulties encountered by older children in coping with the formal rules of mathematics could be prevented if teachers built upon the children's current mathematical understanding and methods of computation. If children are unable to recognize the connections between their intuitive approaches and the ways in which teachers demonstrate calculations, they are likely to feel uncomfortable with both methods and lose confidence in their ability to do mathematics. Ginsburg *et al.* (1997: 201) suggest that although many children have good informal mathematical skills on entry to school, this does not necessarily predict success at school. They suggest that this failure stems at least in part from the 'system of schooling'. Bryant (1997: 67) explores the relationship between what children know about mathematics before they go to school and the extent to which they understand school mathematics. Although he concludes that we do not have a clear answer to this question, he suggests that before starting school children 'have a good understanding of what is involved in sharing' but that their 'grasp of the number of number words . . . seems very shaky indeed'. Despite this, division is not required to be introduced into the teaching of mathematics until Year 3 (DfEE 1999) while the focus in the foundation stage is on addition and subtraction.

This is not to suggest that division should be part of the foundation stage curriculum but it is to suggest that even if the data which Bryant seeks were available, practitioners should use as their starting point what they know of the children they teach. Carraher *et al.* (1991: 234) write:

We do not dispute whether school maths routines can offer richer and more powerful alternatives to maths routines which emerge in non-school settings. The major question appears to centre on the proper pedagogical point of departure i.e. where to start. We suggest that educators should question the practice of treating mathematical systems as formal subjects from the outset and should instead seek ways of introducing these systems in contexts which allow them to be sustained by human daily sense.

Mathematical teaching should reflect, explore and above all link with children's everyday experiences. Perhaps young children's interest in sharing is linked to Paley's (1980) view that fairness is one of their three motivations!

Probably the most difficult and yet most important links are those between everyday and formal mathematical strategies and language. This has been increasingly recognized but it is not an easy process. Practitioners need to explore ways of supporting the necessary learning, rather than simply setting out to teach what is stipulated in curriculum documents. We, as adults, must make connections between our observations of children and what they need to learn. As Pound and Gura (1997: 25) state:

> Those involved in early childhood education [need] to . . . understand how the intuitive and informal languages of early learning can be connected with the more formal languages or disciplines of the later years.

Social and cultural aspects of mathematical learning and development

As we saw in Chapter 1, culture plays an important part in young children's mathematical development. The role of mathematics in the life of the family, its significance within the media, the ways in which it is represented in the language of the home, and the opportunities which a child has to experience weight, time, length, distance or money all contribute to the way in which a child develops mathematically.

Ginsburg et al. (1997: 201) have researched the differences in achievement amongst different cultural groups. They conclude that 'some children begin well and enjoy advantages that may accelerate mathematics learning' while 'other preschool children begin with adequate intellectual ability but eventually perform poorly in school'. This is of course interesting to practitioners. Of particular interest to British practitioners, for example, might be their suggestion that 'African-Americans do not, as a group, realize their potential in school' since it very much echoes the findings of Tizard et al. (1988) a decade earlier in relation to the achievement of young black children in London.

Ginsburg et al. (1997: 201) suggest that Japanese children may be achieving well in mathematics because they are 'born into a culture favouring quantitative activity'. However, some important information may have been overlooked. Japanese pre-school education has over many years placed a heavy emphasis on physical competence and risk-taking (Walsh 2004) and the sense of independence and agency which this produces may be the key to their success. Similarly, the National Numeracy Project team produced a video (NNP 1997) which included work in a Hungarian nursery. It was seen as offering a useful model to British practitioners since mathematical attainment there is among the highest in Europe. The children do not start school until they are aged 6, so the children in the nursery are the equivalent of British Year 1 children. The video explains that Hungarian nursery-aged children have a largely unstructured day with long periods of play broken only by their daily structured 45-minute period of mathematical activity as a whole class. The NNP attributes Hungary's success to the structured session. An equally good hypothesis is that it is the delayed start to formal education and the long periods of play which create the foundation for later mathematical achievement.

Merttens (1997) emphasizes the role of adults in encouraging children to make connections with their peers – to link into one another's mathematical understanding. She draws attention to 'teaching on the rug' (Merttens 1997: 14) and suggests that the interactive processes allow children to imitate and respond to the mathematical thinking of others. She concludes: 'Stories and rhymes have long been a part of teachers' "rug"' repertoire. It is good that maths is now seen that way as well.' Montessori (1912) also stressed the importance of helping children to link their ideas. She emphasized the value of the criticisms which children can make of one another, without the stress and anxiety which similar comments from adults would induce.

While accepting the importance of interactions between children, the issue of sitting on the carpet should not be glossed over. The introduction of the literacy and numeracy strategies (DfEE 1998, DfEE 1999) led far too many practitioners to have groups of very young children sitting on the carpet for far too long. Young children are naturally active (Doherty and Bailey 2003) and while practitioners may see immense value in talking to them in a large group, the difficulties which this poses for them should be considered:

- Keeping a large group together for significant periods of time requires that they sit still and this is difficult and distracting for children who are still learning to control their muscles.
- Large group activities do not permit children to talk much. Young children need time and opportunity to talk about things that interest them and this is not easy in a big group. In quarter of an hour of group time, even if the adults said nothing (which is highly unlikely), children would only have half a minute each in which to speak.

- The levels of discomfort associated with sitting cramped, in a large group, with little opportunity to contribute will do nothing to make what Ruth Merttens calls 'teaching on the rug' a positive experience.

This is not to say that good things cannot come out of group times but the size of group, age of child and length of time they are asked to sit should be key factors in deciding when and how to use group periods. The value of such sessions for children who have particular learning needs or those who are in the early stages of learning English should also be considered very carefully.

There is one further area which should be considered. Babies are born imitators (see for example Murray and Andrews 2000) and their ability to imitate the facial expressions of those around them within minutes of birth is said to be due to the presence of mirror neurons (Blakemore and Frith 2005). The same elements of the brain are activated when we undertake a physical activity and when we see someone else engaged in action. The role of mirror neurons appears to be to enable us to feel empathy with others. It is however particularly useful in considering how best to support children with motor problems which prevent them moving freely. Watching other children moving in, out, through and over equipment enables their brains to be stimulated in ways which help them to benefit from some of the experiences they themselves are unable to take part in.

Positive dispositions

Since most people do not expect to enjoy mathematics it is difficult for them to pass on to children a positive disposition towards learning and thinking mathematically. Research into many areas of expertise (Pound and Harrison 2003) now shows us that many people who are good at things, from remembering strings of unrelated numbers to being a concert pianist, are good at those things because they spend more time doing them. If we want children to be good at mathematics we have to encourage them to enjoy it – we all find it easier to spend time on things we enjoy!

Gifford (2005a: 113) reminds early childhood practitioners of the importance of developing and maintaining children's confidence if they are to be successful in mathematics. She underlines the 'need to monitor their attitudes towards maths and number from an early age, and to guard against passing negative attitudes on to the children'. She comments – as do others, including Munn and Schaffer (1993) – on the fact that early childhood educators often show less interest in developing numeracy than literacy. She suggests (Gifford 1995: 101) that this difficulty could be overcome by helping them to become more aware of and more interested in the underlying cognitive strategies which children use.

Children's disposition to learning mathematics is also inextricably linked to emotions and experiences. Brown (1996) reminds us that when an experience carries a powerful emotional charge it can become unconsciously attached to our mathematical knowledge. This may be positive, but when it is not, it can form a barrier to learning. Walkerdine (1989) provides a comment on an area of mathematics which carries emotional overtones for many of us. She reminds us of its implications for children from different socioeconomic circumstances:

> Different children will have different attitudes to money. 'Counting pennies' may have different meanings – for some a grim reality, for others a casual game of let's pretend. Using money as a metaphor for number in classrooms may be sometimes more problematic than is supposed. The paradox is that those children who understand about money precisely because lack of it is important in their family life may not find it easy, when money is invoked . . . It is ironic that this transition is likely to be smoother for those children who already have a more abstract notion of money – one which is not linked so closely in their lives to rent, food, labour and so on.

'Mathematics is for me!'

> We can influence young children's keenness to learn mathematics by making the tasks they do of interest to them . . . by showing that we really think maths is important and fun and that it is therefore good to be a person who likes mathematics.
>
> (Clemson and Clemson 1994: 19)

Fun is never a sufficient reason for including something in an educational programme, but it is nonetheless essential to early learning. Unless the things we want children to learn are important to them, they will not be remembered. There is another essential ingredient in developing a disposition to learn something – relevance, not only to our context but also to our self-image. Claxton (1997) points out that if information does not fit with our image of who we are, we find it more difficult to respond to it. He cites a study in which adults were asked to role-play being an airline pilot. As part of the preparation, the subjects were given an eye test. During the pretend flying session, the same test materials were used but were integrated into the simulation. Many subjects showed greater visual acuity in play than in tests – demonstrating the strength of Vygotsky's (1978) claim that playful situations enable children to operate at their most skilful. As Aubrey (1994: 37) reminds us, 'drama offers people the opportunity to show they know more than they think they know'.

Play has several important functions in mathematics, as in all areas of learning. When we encourage children to play shops, to dress dolls in appropriate-sized clothing, to fill up pretend cars with litres of make-believe petrol, we are promoting the function of play which helps children to understand the cultural role of these activities. Children's block play, their exploration through play of the relationship between different lengths of blocks, is mathematical. Similarly, play with sand, water and malleable materials can provide opportunities for children to explore mass, volume and capacity. However, we provide these activities not only in order to promote mathematical learning but also because they are rich learning contexts where children can reflect on previous experience and consolidate their current understanding.

Summary

Language offers a useful model for learning successfully. The learning of our first language remains useful throughout our lives, is pleasurable and is not associated with anxiety. More recent neuroscientific findings have strengthened and underlined the importance of the social, emotional and cultural aspects of learning. Mathematical learning will be more successful if we can learn from these lessons. Learning to think relies on an ability to represent ideas in a variety of ways, beginning with physical ways of knowing. Translation and connections between different modes of representation also aid thought. Above all, young children have to be excited and stimulated in order to learn. The task of learning is easy when we *want* to understand and find out more.

Playfulness is essential to human development (Greenfield 1996); and this is especially true of young children's need to make and establish connections. The essence of creativity and innovation (both artistic and scientific) is the making of unusual or unexpected links – playful connections. Those who were the pioneers of the early childhood tradition in Britain understood that time and space were essential ingredients for playing about with ideas (McMillan 1930). Claxton (1997) underlines the importance of speculation, ruminating – in short, taking time to think and learn.

A *curriculum to promote mathematical thinking*

Those who work with young children have a complex task in seeking to create and implement a curriculum which draws on the body of knowledge and insights which is known as mathematics while at the same time recognizing and nurturing the learning abilities of little children. The demands of universities, the teachers of older children, employers and anxious parents can be loud and vociferous, while children's learning needs can be invisible to all but the well-informed observer. Early childhood educators have a grave responsibility to make sure that what Alexander (1997) has termed 'the imperatives of early childhood' are not lost among the noisy demands for early achievement. What looks like greater achievement in the short term may not always prove to be so in the longer term. In setting out to create a curriculum designed to promote mathematical thinking we might ask ourselves at least three questions.

- **Is doing this particular activity going to be in children's long-term interests?** As Lilian Katz reminds us: 'Just because they *can* does not mean they *should*!' Little children can learn to do formal sums but that does not mean that they should – or that it would be in their long-term interests to do so. They can sit quietly colouring worksheets, but they may be learning that mathematics is boring!
- **Am I teaching something which will have to be unlearnt at a later date if the child is to make further progress?** It is all too easy, perhaps particularly when practitioners lack confidence in their own abilities, to give answers that gloss over a current difficulty but

which, in terms of the mathematics that children will encounter later, are only at best half truths. Indeed, such responses can sometimes be completely untrue! Perhaps you can remember a primary school teacher saying to you, 'Five take away seven – you can't do that.' But of course you can! Negative numbers, bank statements and time all rely on being able to do so! It is clear that we quite often take away seven when we only had five to spare.

Similarly Thumpston (1994: 111) reminds teachers of her concern about 'successful short-term outcomes at the expense of true mathematics education'. In order to count we must learn by heart, inside out and back to front, the names of all the numbers. The process we use for this is a short-term one, sometimes called an *instrumental* schema (Clemson and Clemson 1994: 18, citing Skemp): we learn by habit – through saying the names, over and over again. However, we must also learn to reflect on or think about our learning (*relational* schemas) if it is to have long-term value. Of course, children must develop both kinds of approach. We cannot count unless we know the counting names thoroughly. But neither can we apply mathematical knowledge unless we *think*. If educators give weight only to instrumental approaches, children will lose both confidence in their ability to operate at a more reflective level and recognition of the need to do so.

- **Am I failing to teach aspects of the subject which children will need to support their understanding in the long-term?** In considering the content of a curriculum designed to promote mathematical thinking in young children, the body of knowledge considered appropriate must be interwoven with elements which will lead to successful learning in the future.

Claxton (1997: 215) calls these the 'content curriculum' and the 'learning curriculum'. The latter, he says, teaches

> about learning itself: what it is; how to do it; what counts as effective or appropriate ways to learn; what [children] . . . are like as learners; what they are good at and what they are not . . . The learning society requires . . . an educational system which equips all young people – not just the academically inclined – to deal with uncertainty.

Bruce (2005b: 266) reminds us that modern societies need flexible adults and that neglecting the needs of society by not ensuring that play is part of the school's agenda is likely to lead to a society in which people 'are not able to problem solve, persevere, concentrate, (or) be flexible and adaptive'.

If children are not encouraged to think for themselves, to make choices and decisions, to reflect, to tolerate uncertainty from a very early age, their ability to do so at a later stage will be hampered. These are things which have to be learnt – they are best learnt by being nourished rather than censored. In the light of recent, extensive studies of the brain (Claxton 1997; Greenfield 1996), it seems clear that a broad early experience in relation to the content curriculum will, in opening up channels of thought, aid future learning. In ensuring that children's awareness of the world of mathematics around them is aroused early, adults can help to keep active in their brains the possibilities of all that mathematics entails. Greenfield (1996: 75) states that 'well-used connections [in the brain] encourage further development and sophistication . . . Seldom-used links soon fade.' Play, with its combination of repetition, trial and error and pleasure, is the means by which children make sure that the connections are kept alive and active.

The content curriculum: fields of mathematics

If the curriculum is regarded as the total experience which young children undergo, their feelings, senses, things seen and heard, smelled and tasted – in short, as everything from which they learn in the earliest years – it is clear that the notion of a content curriculum (the knowledge that children accrue) is much less important than that of a learning curriculum (the processes or skills which they learn). However, to the lay person mathematics is essentially about its content – numbers, geometry and so on. Parents and carers do stress numbers and, from babies' first days, use counting as an integral part of their interaction with them. Many of the traditional and improvised rhymes and songs which are so crucial to development in the first year of life are based on counting, positional language and patterns. Everyday experiences form the basis of all future learning, and young children, not just in the first year or two, are learning all the time. As seen in Chapter 1, much of what they learn in these first months and years will contribute to their future mathematical understanding.

The publication of the *Curriculum Guidance for the Foundation Stage* (QCA 2000) followed that of the National Numeracy Strategy (DfEE 1999). Although the introduction of the foundation stage was helpful in clarifying the fact that legislation applying to Key Stage 1 did not apply to children in reception classes, its impact was diluted by the fact that many schools had set up whole school plans which included reception classes and were loath to make yet more changes. Political jockeying continued for some time – as evidenced by the publication of a pack of *Mathematical Activities for the Foundation Stage* (DfES 2002), with the apparent purpose of demonstrating that not only reception classes but what went on in nursery classes and other early years settings ought to follow the requirements of the National Numeracy Strategy.

The activities outlined in the pack seemed to ignore the foundation stage guidance about the need to maintain a balance of adult-directed and child-initiated activities, and offered a heavily adult–led diet. The introduction of the Primary National Strategy (DfES 2003) has improved the situation further since the work of the literacy and numeracy and the foundation stage teams at national level has been given equal status. This development coupled with a national focus on transition from the Foundation Stage to Key Stage 1 has relieved much of the pressure felt by reception class teachers. In fact it has led to some guidance for teachers in Year 1 classes in which the need for a better balance of adult-led and child-initiated activity is emphasized (see for example London Borough of Lewisham nd).

Historical factors in this country have led to a situation where an early years curriculum that does not explicitly include a subject called mathematics is unthinkable. This is however not the case in many other countries. In New Zealand, for example, Te Whariki (Ministry of Education 1996), the highly influential early years curriculum, has five main aims (well-being, belonging, contribution, communication and exploration) which do not explicitly include mathematics. In Britain, the six areas of learning in the foundation stage proposed by QCA (2000) has been amended in Scotland (http://www.ltscotland.org.uk/earlyyears/resources/publications/ltscotland/framechildren3to5.asp). Mathematics is no longer a separate area of learning but has been included in 'Knowledge and Understanding of the World'. In these and in many other cases the absence of a named area of the curriculum does not mean that children are not supported in learning mathematics but does perhaps mean that staff feel more able to tackle both content and learning aspects of the curriculum. In this section, the content areas of mathematics are drawn from the requirements of the early learning goals (QCA 2000) and the National Numeracy Strategy (DfEE 1999) and are number; calculating; shape, space and measures.

Number

In their dealings with little children, most adults place some stress on numbers – both ordinal (denoting position in a sequence: first, second . . .) and cardinal (the quantity of objects in a set or group).

Learning numbers by heart is vital – counting is similar to singing a song or reciting a familiar rhyme. Once one imagines oneself trying to recite every other word of a poem or song, or beginning somewhere in the middle, it becomes clear why it is so vital to know the order of the counting words inside out! It also becomes clear why children can have such difficulties in undertaking that which once learnt seems so simple. Reciting number names in the correct order (stable-order principle) is, of course, not enough. In order to count children have also to learn that:

- everything is only counted once and that for each object one number name is used (one-to-one principle)
- the last number name that you say stands for the size of the set (cardinal principle)
- any items can be counted whether similar or dissimilar (abstraction principle)
- items can be counted in any order so long as you apply the one-to-one and stable order principles.

(Pound 2004, citing Gelman and Gallistel 1978)

As if this were not difficult enough, counting is made even more difficult by the fact that in everyday language we use numbers in many different ways. When we are buying eggs we usually are specific. If we say six we mean six – we would not be happy with a box containing five or even with a seventh squashed into the box. However, when we talk about five minutes, we might mean three or fifteen. We talk about something being about five miles or about £10. Even more confusingly, when asked the question how far somewhere is, how often do we respond by saying half an hour or twenty minutes? A question of distance responded to with information about time!

First and second sound very different from *one and two* but this difficulty is compounded when we consider that in a road with odd and even numbered houses on opposite sides of the street, the third house might actually have the number 5 or 6 on its door. When numbers are used in the context of measurement even more issues arise. Very large numbers are often involved and those numbers may have no tangible relationship with what the child is handling. No wonder the children described in Chapter 1 had such difficulty in measuring length – at least with length it might be possible to identify 3 centimetres by placing three 1 centimetre cubes side by side. But what about the 250 grammes mentioned on the toothpaste tube? Even if you put the tube onto a pair of scales, the number 250 will not be registered since the tube itself gives additional weight.

In addition to all that children have to make sense of numbers that have no numerical value – buses, phone numbers, PIN numbers and so on. A number 43 bus is not smaller or earlier than a number 56. No wonder children are so interested in large numbers – there is so much to puzzle over. We should also remember that in written formats numbers and letters are often used interchangeably although they are in fact two different symbol systems. This is clearly not insurmountable since children seem to manage it pretty effectively but it offers just another little challenge. So it becomes increasingly clear that what might seem to the lay person a very simple process, counting and the number system is in fact very complex.

Fortunately there are also a number of factors which make counting easy for us. The first is that our brains are hard-wired for mathematics (Ramachandran and Blakeslee 1999). This is demonstrated in the extraordinary abilities which we now know babies to have in the first year of life. This was discussed in Chapter 1 and gives us great insight into the competence of very young children. Devlin (2000) underlines the way in which our brains have shaped and come to understand mathematics. But in addition he comments on the other insights that humans bring to mathematical thinking. We are both able to empathize with others (see section on imitation in Chapter 2) and to reflect on our own thinking. These capabilities, he claims, along with our remarkable ability to think in the abstract and to use symbols are what make us uniquely mathematical.

This is linked to the second factor that makes counting easy for us – namely that the area of the brain which is responsible for what we do with our fingers is next to the area of the brain which is responsible for counting (Ramachandran and Blakeslee 1999). Thus it is no accident that we so often use our fingers for counting – the use of the symbol (the fingers) reinforces the counting and vice versa. The third factor makes yet another link. All the counting rhymes we sing with accompanying actions in order to teach children to count or at least say the number names in order are reinforcing the learning by:

● using music which all around the world is used to make things easy to remember (Pound and Harrison 2003)
● using finger actions to support both the music and the memorization of numbers (Pound and Harrison 2003)
● creating the 'mass action' (Carter 1999) which stimulates the brain for learning
● promoting the fun and enjoyment which creates a positive chemistry in the brain to support learning (Eliot 1999).

Calculating

Number goes well beyond counting and involves a wide range of operations, many of which are familiar to children in their everyday lives – one more, only three more, fair shares, none left, doubling, halving and estimating. Money has particular significance and clear characteristics with the possibility of exploring exchange and the possibility of gaining five or ten brown coins in exchange for just one small silver one.

One of the difficulties often encountered by young children relates to 'counting on'. As described in Chapter 1, some of the children who were willing to subitize once they had left the nursery seemed to be able to identify large numbers at a glance (Macnamara 1996). They described being able to do this by holding one number in their heads and counting on the remaining group. So, for example, a child able to identify ten dots at one glance might describe 'seeing' seven and adding three more. The fact that so many children who had demonstrated an ability to subitize in the nursery seemed unable to do so in the primary school seems to be linked to the heavy emphasis placed on counting once children enter statutory schooling. It seems important to create a balance between encouraging children to guess how many (subitizing) and checking accurately. If we never let children's guesses stand they will have no confidence in their ability to estimate and will cease to see it as an important strategy in school mathematics. It will, in turn, undermine their capacity to count on – which requires holding a number in your head.

Butterworth (2005) suggests that subsequent difficulties in calculation may arise from a failure in understanding of numerosity. Since this appears on balance to be an innate ability demonstrated in the studies of subitizing, this makes the difficulty faced by some children in learning to calculate difficult to explain. Butterworth explains them by suggesting that failure is 'heavily influenced by the educational practices the child undergoes'.

It should be noted here that Steffe (2004: 236) regards counting on as 'non-teachable'. He states that in his experience 'a demonstration of how to count on is rarely effective'. He adds that if children appear to learn from demonstration it is because they were on the cusp of doing so. Overall Steffe's position is that mathematics in the early years is best taught by first finding out what children can do – or the mathematics of children as he calls it. For him this will demand an understanding of what children might do – the kinds of development that may be seen but it is an even more demanding process. He writes (2004: 235):

Constructing a mathematics of children empowers mathematics teachers in a way that is not possible when the focus is on teaching a pre-determined and a priori mathematics curriculum. There, the focus in often on transferring the teacher's mathematical knowledge from the head of the teacher to the heads of children by means of the words of the language. In contrast, the mathematics of children emerges from within children and it must be constructed by children.

This view contrasts with that of Peter Bryant (1997: 67) who urges that:

If there are connections between children's pre-school mathematical experience and the progress that they eventually make in mathematics lessons at school, we need to know what these are so that we can prepare children for learning mathematics.

The notion of 'a mathematics of children' lies much closer to what is known and understood about teaching young children. Steffe's (2004: 221, citing the National Council of Teachers of Mathematics in the United States 1998) view is that since 'young children make sense of the world by reasoning and problem-solving . . . teachers should recognize that young children think in ways that can be sophisticated'. Of course we want children to learn particular aspects of mathematics but a good practitioner knows that he or she is not dealing with someone who knows nothing of mathematics. The idea that we are *preparing* children for learning mathematics is an outmoded one – we are in fact (or should be if teaching is to be effective) promoting the development which began when they were born. Mathematics does not just exist within the classroom – it is part of life and teaching must acknowledge and harness this. Although legislation requires that particular things are taught, practitioners must ensure that they are effectively learned and this is more likely to be the case when teaching builds on children's current understanding.

Shape, space and measurement

The value of exploring shape and space in early childhood has long been understood although this does not perhaps chime with the popular view of mathematics which is more likely to equate maths with sums. Over 150 years ago, Friedrich Froebel recognized the importance of helping young children to become aware of the interconnectedness of three dimensional shapes. He developed structured materials which he described as 'gifts'. In his early career he made use of a large set of around 500 blocks but gradually he introduced structured sets of materials. The first consisted of six small woollen balls. The second gift was a wooden cube, cylinder and sphere, while the third was eight one-inch cubes, which together formed a single two-inch cube. Subsequent gifts were cut from 8-inch cubes and included cubes, cuboids and triangular prisms (Pound 2005).

In the early years of schooling an emphasis is frequently placed on learning the names of two-dimensional shapes but this may not be the easiest starting point for young children. The physical form of three-dimensional shapes allows children to gain a better understanding of what two-dimensional shapes are since faces and sides are more easily identifiable. Two-dimensional shapes are, after all, representations of an aspect of shape. More experience with three-dimensional shapes might have avoided Dean's dilemma in the following example. Six-year-old Dean (Owen and Rousham 1997: 259) has been completing a worksheet which asks him to say how many sides and corners some two-dimensional shapes have. Corners are no problem, but for each shape he has recorded that there are two sides. His teacher questions him:

Teacher: Dean, I'm not sure this is right, is it? Do all these different shapes have two sides?

Dean: (belligerently) Yes.

Teacher: Well, can you get your shapes and show me the two sides?

Dean: (returning with his set of plastic shapes) Look, (holding triangle in one hand and using his other hand to point, he places his index finger in the centre) one . . . (turns shape over) . . . two.

Boys are more likely to have explored areas on wheeled toys and may be more adventurous in climbing. They commonly wander further from carers and are encouraged to take more physical risks. These experiences raise their spatial awareness and give them greater confidence and insight in dealing with problems relating to space and shape. There is a lesson here for all areas of mathematical learning – early experience makes a difference which it is not always easy to quantify or explain but which we skip, not at our peril, but in risk of the life chances of the children for whom we take responsibility.

Measurement is perhaps the area of mathematics in which children may draw most heavily on their everyday experiences. The measurement of length, mass, volume, capacity and even time is part of many day-to-day conversations. Conceptual understanding of different measures develops at different rates but is closely related to children's experience. Mass is commonly believed to be understood later than, for example, length, but conceptual development is closely related to the real-life experiences to which children are exposed in their homes and communities (Rogoff 1990). More complex measures such as area and speed are not generally seen as essential elements of a curriculum for young children. They are, however, measures which crop up in conversation and which some children will have heard talked about – even if not in precise terms. Once again, those things which are important within the child's family and broader culture will be most readily learnt. Like large numbers, such topics are often of great interest to young children!

The National Numeracy Strategy (DfEE 1999) encourages the use of non-standard measuring units. Gifford (1995) challenges this view. She suggests that if 'children use standard units from the beginning . . . they are . . . more likely to get a feel for units and to acquire "benchmarks" for estimating'. This she claims saves time and prevents confusion. In saying this an important aspect of young children's development is overlooked. The fact that children can use the tools and the language given to them does not mean that they have genuinely understood. Carla Rinaldi (1997) writing in *Shoe and Meter* address the concerns that Gifford raises:

> The real problem, then, is not when and how to explain or present standard measuring instruments to children (at what age? in what way?) but rather to ask how we can create the conditions that enable the development of divergent and creative thought: how to sustain the ability and the pleasure involved in comparing ideas with others rather than simply confronting a single idea that is presumed to be 'true' or 'right' (legitimated knowledge, established codes and disciplinary areas). All this is much truer and more important the younger the child is. It is not only a pedagogical and didactic issue, but also one of ethics and values.

Time is a very difficult concept for young children (as it is for many adults). Music and dance offer unique and effective ways for children to learn about them – linking with counting, spatial awareness and positional language. Shape and space, including the language used to describe position, direction and movement are closely linked to physical experience. Since as we saw in Chapter 2 thinking begins with the physical, opportunities to physically experience aspects of shape and space are of fundamental importance.

The learning curriculum: mathematical processes

The younger the child, the more the processes of mathematical learning resemble the processes of all other learning. The idea of any subject focus for babies, for example, is probably laughable and yet there are things which they must learn from the earliest moments in order to become thinking mathematicians. Confidence, independence, risk-taking (essential in estimating and approximating), learning from others and learning from exploration will support their mathematical development, but will also support later learning in other areas of experience, subjects and disciplines. In Table 3.1 the learning dispositions which underpin all effective learning have been outlined (drawn from *Birth to Three Matters* (Sure Start 2002); *Curriculum Guidance for the Foundation Stage* QCA 2000; Dowling 2005; Carr 2001). Some general characteristics have been highlighted and their relationship to aspects of mathematical development identified.

While there are a vast number of processes involved in learning to think mathematically in this chapter the focus will be on four aspects, which may be thought of as the cornerstones around which foundations can be built. These four vital aspects are:

- identifying pattern
- problem-finding
- guessing
- learning to think in the abstract.

In considering the learning curriculum we need to bear in mind that:

- Children can learn mathematics even in activities that do not seem to be primarily mathematical.
- Children tend to make little spontaneous use of their knowledge of numbers because, as a number of writers have warned, numeracy is often given less emphasis than literacy in many homes and early years settings (Gifford 2005b; Munn 1994; Rogers 1997).
- Even those aspects which appear to be most specific to mathematics, such as recognizing and using numbers up to 10, are most effectively learnt in contexts such as role play and relevant real-life events where children are actively encouraged to draw on their previous experiences.

Searching for patterns

Searching for patterns and relationships is fundamental to all mathematics. Mathematics is full of patterns and is fundamentally concerned with differences and similarities. Burton (1994: 13) writes that she finds it 'impossible to think about learning or using mathematics in any other way than by patterning or by looking for relationships'. Even when the patterns and relationships are not explicitly drawn to children's attention, they themselves seek to make sense of mathematics, like all other

Table 3.1 The importance of positive dispositions in mathematical development

Sure Start Unit 2002	QCA 2000	Dowling 2005	Carr 2001	Relevance to mathematical development
Connecting ideas and understanding the world	Interested, excited and motivated	Motivation Problem-solving	Taking an interest	Making connections between: • mathematics at home and at school or other early years setting • mathematics across the curriculum and across areas of provision Learning more effectively because of being excited and interested to learn Children finding their own problems which sustain interest and motivation
Realisation of own individuality Becoming able to trust and rely on own abilities Responding to the world imaginatively	Confident to initiate	Curiosity Creativity	Taking responsibility	Confidence comes from a strong sense of self and creative, imaginative responses arise when children feel secure enough to act independently. Being willing to guess requires confidence.
Acquiring social confidence and competence Being a sociable and effective communicator Being a confident and competent language user	Confident to speak in a familiar group		Being involved Communicating with others	Communication and thought are said to be synonymous (Goldschmied and Selleck 1996). When we support children in becoming confident communicators we are supporting their ability to think.

Listening and responding to the language of others			
Understanding and being understood			
Being able to make choices	Maintain attention, concentrate	Perseverance Reflection	Persisting with difficulty	Problem-finding and solving, and identifying patterns can sometimes require quiet reflection and a willingness to persevere when things don't seem to be going well.

areas of learning, by trying to identify the rules which will help them to understand. Thus Burton continues: 'Patterns and relationships not only describe mathematics, they also give us a way of looking at children's learning of mathematics.'

In referring to the human mind as a pattern recognizer, Devlin (2000: 61) goes further. He explains as follows:

> The patterns and relationships studied by mathematicians occur everywhere in nature: the symmetrical pattern of flowers, the often complicated pattern of knots, the orbits swept out by planets as they move through the heavens, the pattern of spots on a leopard's skin, the voting pattern of a population, the pattern produced by the random outcomes in a game of dice or roulette, the relationship between the words that make up a sentence, the pattern of sound that we recognize as music. Sometimes the patterns are numerical and can be described using arithmetic – voting patterns for example. But often they are not numerical – for example, patterns of knots and symmetry patterns of flowers have little to do with numbers.
>
> (Devlin 2000: 73)

To identify pattern we may use a range of strategies. Athey (1990: 41) talks about seriation (which she describes as being about seeing differences between things) and classification (described as seeing similarities). She writes:

> Seriation and classification have their origin in early actions applied to a wide range of objects and, later, to events. The common-sense world contains sufficient information to feed seriation structures such as size, height, weight, strength, temperature, porosity, number and so on.

Pattern is an aspect of the mathematics curriculum which is frequently under-represented in the early years. The *Curriculum Guidance for the Foundation Stage* (QCA 2000) includes a single goal which states that by the end of the foundation stage children should be able to 'talk about, recognise and recreate simple patterns'. This simple statement masks a complexity which exists in an aspect of mathematics which offers fertile ground for the development of wonder and excitement as children explore the patterns and relationships which exist within number, shape and space. It is reassuring to see a reference to pattern in *Birth to Three Matters* (Sure Start Unit 2002) as an aspect of becoming a competent learner, making connections.

Too often, the exploration of pattern with young children in nurseries, reception classes and playgroups is too narrowly confined to activities such as bead-threading. Much is made in the relevant mathematical development literature of the difficulties which young children have in recognizing and copying patterns. In her systematic and accessible study Montague-Smith (2002), for example, draws attention to the difficulties demonstrated by young children in copying bead patterns, demonstrated in the work of Piaget. Although from about the age of 2 they are able to assemble the necessary components of a pattern, they apparently still have difficulty in reproducing it right through to 4 or 5 years of age.

To accept this interpretation is to ignore the rich potential of children's day-to-day lives and the wide variety of situations in which patterns exist. At a very early stage, babies are attracted by patterns – particularly those that have similarities with the human face. Even the youngest babies can quickly establish an understanding of the relationship between the sound of a spoon on a dish and being fed. Over time they can develop a keen understanding of the relationship between events – just try missing parts of a well-loved story! Cumulative stories, songs and rhymes with a repeating pattern are readily recalled by young children.

The apparent discrepancy between Piaget's finding and children's obvious abilities may be accounted for by the relevance of the activities. Bead patterns do not match up with the *enthusiasms* of children of this age. If we really want to know about and foster young children's understanding of pattern and relationships we should look to the patterns of the day, week and year, in music, stories, house numbers and so on.

Identifying relationships involves categorizing and classifying. Gifford (1995) reminds us that 'the "sorting, ordering and matching" curriculum has been discredited'. While this is to be welcomed, the word has sadly not been spread to the many early years settings where worksheets and sets of plastic shapes abound. Too often children are given tasks that they can already do and which are presented as isolated activities, unrelated to anything else. They are too often justified as necessary precursors to the 'real' mathematics which will come later. Merttens (1996: 20) quotes the following conversation between a parent and child:

P: What did you do today?
C: Well I spent a long time sorting out Mrs Williams' animals, but when I finished she tipped them all back in a box.

We should not of course ignore children's own drive to sort and match things. The persistent concerns that were discussed in Chapter 2 that arise out of schemas may be the driving force but other passions also lead children to sort and match. Two year old Maria enjoyed playing with a new farm set which had arrived in a divided box – her play with it was dominated by taking the animals out and replacing them in the appropriate spaces.

As Merttens (1996: 22) reminds us, 'Mathematics is primarily an activity of the mind, closely bound up with the social context in which it takes place.' Young children are most likely to be able to recognize pattern, differences and similarities in the things with which they are most concerned and interested. As Gopnik *et al.* (1999: 85) remind us, all of us and not just young children 'look beyond the surfaces of the world and try to infer its deeper patterns'. That drive is the only real starting point and educators working with young children must ensure that it is allowed to be so.

Problem-finding/problem-solving

> Mathematical know-how is the ability to solve problems – not merely routine problems but problems requiring some degree of independence, judgement, originality and creativity.
>
> (Pólya 1957).

Problem-solving or problem-finding, like pattern seeking, is something humans seem to need to do. Gopnik *et al.* (1999: 85) emphasize the way in which:

> When we're presented with a puzzle, a mystery, a hint of a pattern, something that doesn't quite make sense, we work at it until we find a solution. In fact we intentionally set ourselves such problems, even the quite trivial ones . . . like crossword puzzles, video games, or detective stories.

It is this drive, shared by even very young children, to find problems to solve which makes the element of problem-finding at least as important as problem-solving. In real-life situations they show remarkable persistence, learning over time to use a series of actions to solve a particular problem. Toddlers put a great deal of time and energy into solving problems and practise the steps involved with diligence. Adults who have helped young children to solve a problem are sometimes frustrated when the child immediately recreates the situation that they were struggling with. The grunts and squeals begin again as the child wrestles anew with the challenge they have set themselves.

Why is 3-month-old Lawrence so anxious to turn over that he struggles and struggles with no apparent incentive? Why does 15-month-old Izzi push herself to the point of exhaustion in her determination to not simply push her buggy over loose gravel (a difficult enough task) but to push it loaded with the wooden blocks? The level of engagement and persistence demonstrated by these very young children is the level of perseverance and drive which leads to effective learning. To achieve this, teachers and other practitioners or educators have to build on children's passions or 'persistent concerns' so that children can identify and solve their own problems.

Problem-solving has been characterized (Burton 1994; Thumpston 1994) as one of the core elements in the development of mathematical thinking. Yet it often tends, along with a range of other open-ended activities, to be marginalized – perhaps because of the adults' lack of confidence. Both the National Numeracy Strategy (DfEE 1999) and the early learning goals (QCA 2000) include objectives related to problem-solving but no mention alas of problem-finding!

Children can of course learn from being involved in solving problems which interest or excite them. Children's suggestions for solving problems tell us a great deal about their level of understanding and give us an insight into the power of their 'puzzling minds' (Tizard and Hughes 1984). The responses of 3- and 4-year-olds in a nursery school asked to suggest how best to empty the sand pit (Pound et al. 1992) range from the relatively pedestrian 'Use a big bucket and take it to the other sand pit' to the ingenious 'Get a saucepan, make a hole in it, put a pipe in, put [it] in to other sandpit and the sand will go in the other sandpit'. Pippie comes up with the fantastic idea of putting all the sand into a chest of drawers which can then be moved along on something slippery. Her suggestion 'What about ice?' is precisely the strategy used by the Chinese to move across their country to Beijing a huge slab of marble which now forms a decorative panel in the Forbidden Palace.

The view that problem-solving requires far more than just good ideas is echoed by a number of writers. Playfulness and creativity go hand in hand, and both are essential ingredients in the problem-solving process (Papousek 1994). The thinking processes that are part of play – deciding, imagining, reasoning, predicting, planning, trying new strategies and recording – turn out to be the very ones that are required for later mathematical thinking (Lewis 1996). Schiro (2004: 57) suggests that discovering problems and their solutions requires insight and intuition. He writes that 'insight is born from blending imaginative and intuitive feeling with intellect'. For him the imaginative and intuitive arise from stories.

Confidence is also vital. Baker (1995: 149) outlines a process developed by teachers in helping children to solve problems, and comments on their 'wholesale agreement about the way in which personal levels of confidence could be enhanced or destroyed depending on the quality of experience and activity undertaken'. The confidence to which Chiu et al.

(1994) draw attention is based on what they term 'resilience'. Learners who face failure with equanimity, who know that they can keep trying and who do not hold too fixed a view of their own potential, are more likely to persevere. Interestingly she identifies 'bright girls' – good at getting right answers – as the least resilient learners.

Claxton (1997: 214) has identified time as a vital element in the problem-solving process. He suggests that it is not really a question of *quantities* of time but rather of taking one's time. He writes:

> The slow ways of knowing will not deliver their delicate produce when the mind is in a hurry. In a state of continual urgency and harassment the brain–mind's activity is condemned to follow its familiar channels. Only when it is meandering can it spread and puddle, gently finding out such fissures and runnels as may exist.

Guessing

Although this section is entitled 'guessing' it refers to a range of abilities which may be called 'estimating', 'predicting', 'approximating' or even 'hypothesizing'. Traditionally, school mathematics has placed an emphasis on getting sums right and guessing has often been frowned upon. In everyday life, accuracy is important in some situations (such as engineering, medicine and rocket science) but in most contexts, we work on approximate figures or informed guesses. We say that we will need about £5 or that we'll only be two minutes.

We rarely need to be entirely accurate, but we often fail to make that clear to children. We need to help them think about when and why we need accuracy and when we do not. In fact humans are not very good at accurate thought – our brains apparently preferring 'fuzzy thinking' (Devlin 2000: 63). In most aspects of life this is an advantage since we are able to make quick judgements based on small amounts of information from which we have identified patterns and made connections. In fact, to be accurate requires our brains to make a supreme effort (Devlin 2000).

Devlin explodes another important myth about accuracy in mathematics when he reports that mathematicians do not arrive at answers to problems by logic but rather by guessing an answer and then trying to find a way to prove it. He claims that:

> Precise, formal reasoning is not required for mathematical discovery. Rather its purposes are verification of things already discovered (or perhaps suspected) . . . The need for formal

verification is a direct consequence of the nature of mathematical discovery (which includes) trial and error, guesswork, intuition, and conversation with others.

(ibid: 252)

Claxton (2000: 33) shares this view (citing John Stuart Mills) in saying that 'the truths known by intuition are the original premises from which all others are inferred'. He suggests that intuition is a learning process and involves expertise, judgement, attentiveness and reflection on experience. Schiro (2004: 57) also echoes this view. Citing Poincaré he suggests that 'it is by logic that we prove but by intuition that we discover'. He goes on to describe a teacher, seeking to develop mathematical understanding through story as wanting

> to help children know mathematics on the intuitive level where 'they know it in their bones'. Once they have an intuitive understanding of and feel for mathematics, they can then move on to understand it at a more abstract, generalized objective level.

The term 'guessing' is sometimes used disparagingly (see for example Gifford 1995) often being seen as a random process. But logic and reason are not the only ways in which humans think. The intuitive or informed guess is as worthy as a prediction, hypothesis or estimate.

Because in schools we focus so much on accuracy, children are often loath to estimate. They are afraid of getting it wrong and frequently don't understand the difference between being nearly right and way off beam. But in fact this is precisely what children need to be able to do if they are to use calculators effectively and to make sound judgements about mathematics in everyday life. It is as important to know, for example, that 9×7 will be less than 10×7 or 70 as to be able to recite that $9 \times 7 = 63$.

The other important aspect of approximating mathematically answers in everyday life is its relevance. The answer we come up with matters if we're playing darts or getting change from a shopkeeper in a way that plastic cubes in the classroom can never matter. If we talk about estimation, approximation or hypotheses, this process sounds more laudable but actually (whatever you call it) it is an essential part of mathematics. It is the link between formal and informal mathematics; it is the process which keeps the learner from coming up with ridiculous answers.

Learning to think in the abstract

Despite the fact that mathematics is rooted in real life, it is a very abstract subject. Devlin (2000) suggests that it is the *most* abstract subject but since he is a mathematician we may choose to discount his view as biased. We can support children in developing the ability to think in the abstract by three main strategies. These are:

- developing imagination
- creating mental images
- representing ideas.

Developing imagination

As we saw in Chapter 2, there is renewed interest in the role of play and imagination in developing the ability to think in the abstract. This is in part linked to creativity and to what has been termed 'possibility thinking' (Craft 2001). We should not however underestimate the importance of imaginative play in its own right. Jenkinson (2001, quoting Pearce 1997) uses language close to that which Devlin uses in describing the development of abstract thought (see Chapter 2):

> Imagination means creating images that are not present to the senses. All of us exercise this faculty every day and every night . . . the whole crux of human intelligence hinges on this ability of mind.
>
> . . . nature has not programmed error into the genetic system and . . . the child's preoccupation with fantasy and imagination is vital to development.

Imaginative play is vital to mathematical development as well as all other aspects of learning and development. Practitioners offer many experiences to children which are focused on imaginative play areas but unless

- children are in charge of their play
- are focusing on their own interests
- are enjoying the experience
- are free from external expectations

the activities or experiences offered cannot be counted as play (Edgington 2004). They may offer playful teaching opportunities but they cannot take the place of more open-ended play.

Edgington (2004) also suggests that the purpose of play may be to co-ordinate learning through:

- exploration and discovery
- construction
- repeating and practising
- representing
- creating
- imagining
- socializing?

Open-ended, problem-seeking, joyful play has an important role in supporting children's all-round development including their mathematical development.

Creating mental images

Lewis (1996) suggests that conversations and planned activities should encourage children to develop mental images, rather than always relying on concrete apparatus. The seminal work of Martin Hughes (1986a) reminds us that children do not need actual objects to count – with small numbers, even quite young children can imagine them. We do not actually have to present them with two elephants and three more elephants, they can see them in their heads. Activities based on Hughes's tins with small bricks placed inside are a good example of such activities. Over time, beginning with real bricks going into the tin, children developed the ability to imagine the bricks even when none were visible. Numberlines and number squares and the use of fingers or structured apparatus as memory aids can provide the basis for reflective thought – providing visual cues or, in Brown's (1996) term, *metaphors* for thinking.

Williams (1996) also reminds us that numberlines (both washing lines with numbers to peg on and strips up to 10 or even 100) and hundred squares provide important images from which children can work – initially by actually touching each number, then gradually being able to summon up helpful mental images. We might also take Williams's advice and encourage children to draw or otherwise represent their mental images. Fingers, abacuses and structural apparatus can all play a role in supporting the development of mental images, particularly as they provide a physical dimension to memory (Brown 1996; Gifford 2005b; Tacon and Atkinson 1997).

Asking children about the images they see when presented with mathematical ideas can promote mathematical thinking. Even if they do not respond, the question may well trigger thinking which will make their own thinking more transparent to them – children will begin to become aware of their own thinking. Giving praise for explaining methods and emphasizing the variety of methods can encourage children to develop mental strategies. Williams (1996: 38) writes:

> Asking a four-year-old 'How did you work that out?', the reply is often of the kind: 'I just did it'. Perhaps a detailed answer is not necessary: it is enough that we draw their attention to the process of them doing something in their heads.

The specialist use of language can sometimes create unhelpful mental images. The use of language in mathematics does not always correspond to the use made of it in everyday contexts. What does a 5- or 6-year-old conjure up when a teacher talks about 'taking away'? It is unlikely to be subtraction – more likely pizza or chow mein. The language which we use shapes children's thinking and the strategies they choose to use. Specific terms such as 'more' and 'less' may pose difficulties for some children. Walkerdine (1989: 53) gives examples of 4-year-old girls using 'more' in their day-to-day conversation:

C: I want some more.
M: No, you can't have any more, Em.
C: Yes! Only one biscuit.
M: No.
C: Half a biscuit?
M: No.
C: A little of a biscuit?
M: No.
C: A whole biscuit?
M: No.
C: Has you still got some more?
M: Hmm?
C: Have you still got some more?
M: Just enough for today and get some more tomorrow.

Walkerdine's point is that children have little difficulty with understanding 'more' but for them the opposite is not 'less' but 'no more' or 'not as much'. Certainly if a young child does not want carrots, she is rarely in the business of asking for a smaller portion, or less – she is generally clamouring for none at all or, as a last resort, just one.

Introducing the formal language of mathematics in informal or play situations can help children to use and understand the appropriate language at a later stage (Aubrey 1994). If adults use specific mathematical language when talking to children who are playing in the sand or water the vocabulary becomes familiar. Further use of the same words and phrases in imaginative play situations or informal conversation promotes children's understanding of the concepts in question. As play allows children to rehearse aspects of learning, so this informal use of formal language helps children to feel at home with what may otherwise be threatening.

As with other aspects of mathematical development, the starting point must always be the child's current understanding – our efforts must go into helping each child to make the connections which will promote their idiosyncratic personal understanding. The developmentally appropriate curriculum which emerges when we work from children's starting point is most likely to promote their individual understanding. Respect for children's efforts to make sense of the world will in turn help adults to make sense of children's learning needs. The wider the child's experience of using language in a range of contexts and registers, the more likely he or she is to understand the specific use of language for mathematics. A developmentally appropriate curriculum will ensure that children are helped to make links between the languages with which they feel comfortable in communication and the formal language of mathematics. The language we use may be getting in the way of understanding – but it can be used to help children clarify their thinking. Children's use of language may cloud their meaning, but if we listen respectfully, with the expectation that they have worthwhile things to say, then their words can help us to understand their meanings (Paley 1990). This in turn can help them to clarify their own thinking.

Representing mathematical ideas

Recording can be useful in promoting thinking. Sensitively used, it can help children to develop awareness of their ways of thinking, to remember things and clarify thinking. It supports the gradual shift from the physical or enactive modes of thinking towards the symbolic. When built on their preferred modes of representation, it can extend the tools for thinking (Egan 1988) available to them. Worthington and Carruthers (2003: 7, citing Whitin *et al.* 1990) suggest that:

> True mathematical literacy must originate not from a methodology, but from a theory of learning: one that views mathematics not as a series of formulas, calculations, or even problem-solving techniques, but as a way of knowing and learning about the world.

Williams (1996: 34) discusses the uses of mathematical mark-making in ways which make human sense to young children, specifically in reception classes. She suggests encouraging children to use a symbol to identify the solution to a problem, giving the example of pricing goods in a shop. Role play is further recommended as a sound context for mathematical mark-making, helping 'children to bridge the gap between a practical activity, mathematical thinking and symbolic recording' in ways which directly draw on their experience. The inclusion of writing materials alongside activities which might generate some mathematical data might also promote recording; for example, rulers in the creative workshop, a numberline in the writing area, clipboards and rulers in the block area, calculators and calendars in the role-play area can encourage children to make mathematical recordings. She also recommends that teachers get into the habit of asking children to keep their own mathematical notes as they work.

Gifford (2005b) makes a similar point, citing nurseries where children are encouraged to keep scores in their games. Some will use conventional numbers, some will use tallies, drawings and some will use entirely idiosyncratic symbols. Like children's invented writing, in the early stages these notes may seem haphazard or indecipherable but over time, given encouragement, relevant situations and appropriate models, children's approximations will approach standard forms. It is also clear that they are not incomprehensible to the children who actually make the marks. The adult's role in demonstrating such strategies is vital and will be discussed in Chapter 5. Worthington and Carruthers (2003: 81) contrast the value given to children's early attempts at mathematical recording with other early representations such as writing and drawing, commenting that 'it is almost as though young children never make mathematical marks'.

As the photo taken in a nursery school (Figure 3.1) reminds us, recording can be made relevant and immediate for young children. In the photo, children are comparing the size of sunflowers to that of paper plates – comparing, observing and discussing. Children at the same school also used lengths of ribbon which they called 'pumpkin-measurers'. The length of the ribbon had been cut to the size of a pumpkin's circumference. The ribbons were used to compare with the size of other objects both live and inanimate. The children recorded directly onto the ribbon – making a mark to show the length and a drawing or symbol to record what it was they had measured. These activities sparked off an interest in both measuring and recording which was long lasting.

In the long run children's mathematical understanding will benefit immensely from the use of standard symbols. They are part of a universal language, they contain a large amount of information in a very compact form and they can give children and parents a keen sense of achievement (Atkinson and Clarke 1992). Unfortunately, the latter benefit is sometimes allowed to override the disadvantages of an inappropriately early introduction to standard notations. This often has the effect of undermining children's confidence, robbing them of any sense of relevance and causing confusion. Walkerdine (1988) underlines the density of mathematical notation. If children are, at a later stage, to understand the wide range of meanings that can be read into a simple number sentence such as 3 + 4 = 7 they will need to have experienced those meanings in a variety of concrete, verbal and mental ways.

Figure 3.1 Learning to record measurement

The requirements of both the early learning goals (QCA 2000) and the National Numeracy Strategy (DfEE 1999) have reduced the pressure on practitioners to introduce formal notation too early. Anghileri (1995: 33) has suggested a five-step sequence towards standard recording which might support practitioners in feeling confident about resisting too early an introduction to formal recording. First, she suggests that learners need to explain their thinking to others. Second, they may be encouraged to demonstrate (or represent) their mental images with objects or drawings. Third, they might be encouraged to record these ideas in written form. Then they might be offered successively short ways of recording, other than in writing, before finally moving to standard notations. It is important to bear in mind the practical experience which must accompany such a process and the role of the adult in demonstrating this kind of thinking without pressurizing the child immediately to do the same. When children are learning to talk, they listen and watch for a long time before they actually make a full contribution to the conversation. We should allow them similar opportunities to see adults and other children recording in a variety of ways.

In addition, the work of a number of researchers has encouraged many teachers to explore children's invented notations (Hughes 1986a; Atkinson 1992; Worthington and Carruthers 2003). Interest in the work on emergent literacy which has been developed over the past twenty to thirty years has led to some explorations of the development of emergent mathematics (Hughes 1986a; Munn 1994; Sinclair 1988). Hughes developed a technique which has come to be known as the 'tins game'. Children were presented with four identical tins with 0, 1, 2 or 3 bricks inside. They were asked to make a mark on the lid of each box to remind them how many bricks were concealed inside. Some examples of children's responses can be seen in Figure 3.2.

While most studies have been conducted in a research context, Gifford (1995) and Atkinson (1992) worked in classrooms. While this has obvious benefits it also has the disadvantage of producing only small samples. Worthington and Carruthers (2003: 84) have drawn on the available evidence and have identified five common forms of graphics (dynamic, pictographic iconic, written and symbolic graphics) which children use in representing mathematical ideas (Table 3.2) and dimensions in which they present them (Table 3.3). They suggest further that these representations may occur in all sorts of play situations and may be seen serving many purposes in children's play and mark-making.

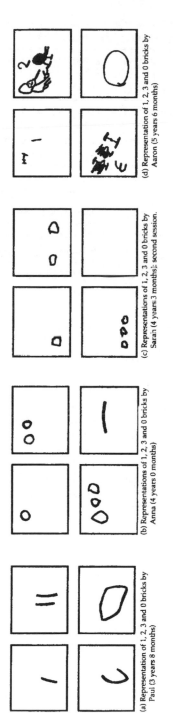

(a) Representation of 1, 2, 3 and 0 bricks by Paul (3 years 8 months)

(b) Representations of 1, 2, 3 and 0 bricks by Anna (4 years 0 months)

(c) Representations of 1, 2, 3 and 0 bricks by Sarah (4 years 3 months): second session.

(d) Representation of 1, 2, 3 and 0 bricks by Aaron (5 years 6 months)

Figure 3.2 (a–d) The bottom right-hand corner of each example shows the child's representation of zero.
Source: Martin Hughes (1986a)

Table 3.2 Forms of graphic representation of mathematical ideas used by young children (based on Worthington and Carruthers 2003)

Form of graphic	Explanation (based on Worthington and Carruthers 2003)	Examples
Dynamic	Marks that are lively and suggestive of action	Pictures that convey a sense of speed with rapid and perhaps chaotic lines criss-crossing indicating the movements of a car
Pictographic	Attempt to represent what they see	A spider with many legs – indicating a lot rather than a specific number
		Drawings of people with many fingers
Iconic	One mark for one object	Tallies or idiosyncratic marks described by (1986a, cited by Worthington and Carruthers: 85) as 'marks of their own devising'. (See Figure 3.2)
		Both Munn (1994) and Sinclair (1988) also describe children using standard numerals in an iconic way i.e. 1, 12, 123, 1234 etc. (representing numbers 1-4).
Written	Words or letter-like marks	Children describe mathematical ideas using a mixture of standard and invented spellings and number- or letter-like symbols.
Symbolic	Standard forms of numerals including some use of symbols such as +	Children begin to use standard numbers and symbols in more conventional forms, although not necessarily wholly accurate.

Table 3.3 Some characteristic types of young children's mathematical graphics (based on Worthington and Carruthers 2003)

Dimensions of mathematical graphics	Explanation (based on Worthington and Carruthers 2003)	Examples
Early play with objects and explorations with marks	Ideas may be represented by a wide range of play e.g. blocks, role-play etc.	See for example Edward's representation of 5 minutes, using blocks described in Chapter 2 (drawn from Gura 1992).
Early written numerals	Referring to marks as numbers	Pages of squiggles etc. described as 'Izzi's numbers' (see also Fig. 3.2)
Numerals as labels	Trains, buses, age	Drawings of buses may be given a specific number (see Chapter 1 Fig. 1.3). Drawings or other graphic representations may be liberally decorated with the child's age – usually 4.
Representations of quantities and counting	Representing e.g. 'hundreds and pounds'	Worthington and Carruthers (2003) offer the example of a child's painting covered in dabs which she describes as 'hundreds and pounds' denoting a large quantity.
Early operations: development of children's own written methods	One of the strengths of the National Numeracy Strategy is its support for children developing their own methods. Worthington and Carruthers offer a wide range of strategies employed by children in representing. Counting continuously Separating sets Exploring symbols Standard symbolic operations with small numbers Calculating with larger numbers, perhaps using jottings	Examples of children's own methods given for subtraction: rubbing out or crossing out pictures; numbers of symbols to show that they have been 'taken away'; circling items to be subtracted; using arrows; drawing a hand 'taking away' the items

These insights are helpful in conveying to practitioners the truly amazing efforts that young children make in order to make sense of difficult symbolic languages. We must remember that young children's errors may not be careless mistakes but intelligent responses which reflect their incomplete knowledge.

Summary

Early access to experiences which will help children to develop aware-ness of all fields of the content curriculum are vital in order to establish channels of thinking. The content must include measurement, shape and space, and patterns and relationships as well as number. Little of the learning curriculum is specific only to mathematics, but where it is it will be most effectively learned in familiar contexts and later applied to more abstract or formal situations. Table 3.4 identifies the development of mathematical learning from the foundation stage into Key Stage 1, linking the outcomes to the learning curriculum.

Table 3.4 The development of mathematical learning, including the content and learning curricula

	Curriculum Guidance for the Foundation Stage (QCA 2000)	*National Numeracy Strategy KS1 (DfEE 1999)*
Content curriculum for mathematical development		
Number	Say and use number names in order in familiar contexts	Count reliably at least 20 objects (Y1)
	Count reliably up to 10 everyday objects	Count on and back in ones from any small number, and in tens from and back to zero (Y1)
	Recognize numerals 1–9	
		Read, write and order numbers from 0 to at least 20; understand and use the vocabulary of comparing and ordering these numbers (Y1)
		Within the range 0–30 say the number that is 1 or 10 more or less than any given number (Y1)

Table 3.4 (*continued*)

	Curriculum Guidance for the Foundation Stage (QCA 2000)	National Numeracy Strategy KS1 (DfEE 1999)
		Count, read, write, order whole numbers to at least 100; know what each digit represents (including 0 as a place holder) (Y2)
		Describe and extend simple number sequences (including odd/even numbers, counting on or back in ones or tens from any two-digit number and so on) (Y2)
Calculating	In practical activities and discussion begin to use the vocabulary involved in addition, subtraction and comparing numbers	Understand the operation of addition, and of subtraction (as 'take away' or 'difference') and use the related vocabulary (Y1)
	Begin to relate addition to combining two groups of objects and subtraction to 'taking away'	Know by heart all pairs of numbers with a total of 10 (Y1)
	Find one more or less than a number from 1 to 10	Understand that subtraction is the inverse of addition; state the subtraction corresponding to a given addition and vice versa (Y2)
		Know by heart all addition and subtraction facts for each number to at least 10 (Y2)
		Use knowledge that addition can be done in any order to do mental calculations more efficiently (Y2)
		Understand the operation of multiplication as repeated addition or as describing an array (Y2)
		Know and use halving as the inverse of doubling (Y2)
		Know by heart facts for the 2 and 10 multiplication tables (Y2)

Table 3.4 (*continued*)

	Curriculum Guidance for the Foundation Stage (QCA 2000)	National Numeracy Strategy KS1 (DfEE 1999)
Shape, space and measures	Use language such as 'greater', 'smaller', 'heavier' or 'lighter' to compare quantities	Compare two lengths, masses or capacities by direct comparison (Y1)
	Use language such as 'circle' or 'bigger' to describe the shape and size of solid and flat shapes	Suggest suitable standard or uniform non-standard units and measuring equipment to estimate, then measure a length, mass or capacity (Y1)
	Use everyday words to describe position	Use everyday language to describe features of familiar 3-D and 2-D shapes (Y1)
		Estimate, measure and compare length, masses and capacities using standard units, suggest suitable units and equipment for such measurements (Y2)
		Read a simple scale to the nearest labelled division, including using a ruler to draw and measure lines to the nearest centimetre (Y2)
		Use the mathematical names for common 2-D and 3-D shapes; sort shapes and describe some of their features (Y2)
		Use mathematical vocabulary to describe position, direction and movement (Y2)

Learning curriculum for mathematical development

Guessing	The guesses or estimations that children make when subitizing are an important part of learning to think mathematically. Estimation needs to be promoted across the curriculum for mathematics – since it underpins all mathematical processes.

Table 3.4 (*continued*)

	Curriculum Guidance for the Foundation Stage (QCA 2000)	*National Numeracy Strategy KS1 (DfEE 1999)*
Identifying patterns	Talk about, recognize and recreate simple patterns: this is the only mention of pattern in teaching children 'the science of patterns' (Devlin 2000). Helping children to be excited about the patterns in numbers, in calculation as well as in relation to shape, space and measures should underpin all mathematical teaching and learning.	At Key Stage 1 pattern remains implicit. Helping children to identify pattern in all aspects of mathematics teaching and learning will enhance achievement and give children a better understanding of what mathematics is and can do.
Thinking in the abstract	In the early stages, abstract thought develops out of the use of the imagination and from learning to see things in the mind that are not visible to the eye. Learning to represent ideas in language, graphics and other forms of recording supports the development of mathematical thinking.	
Problem-solving	Use developing mathematical ideas (about numbers and counting) and methods to solve practical problems Use developing mathematical ideas (about calculating) and methods to solve practical problems Use developing mathematical ideas (about shape, space and measures) and methods to solve practical problems	Use mental strategies to solve simple problems using counting, addition, subtraction, doubling and halving, explaining methods and reasoning orally (Y1). Choose and use appropriate operations and efficient calculation strategies to solve problems, explaining how the problem was solved (Y2).
Problem-finding	The early learning goals (QCA 2000) and National Numeracy Strategy (DfEE 1999) identify problem-solving as an aspect to be developed in mathematical teaching and learning. However, problem-solving can suggest a passive process – problems to be solved given to the children by the teacher. If children are to maintain a positive disposition to mathematics what they actually need to do is to develop a habit of problem-finding. The aim should be for children to *want* to find out more, to be looking for new patterns, anxious to follow up their hunches and so on.	

In their play children learn early a number of thinking skills which are vital to the development of mathematical thinking. The thinking in action which occurs in play forms a rich foundation for the more subject-specific problem-solving, mental imaging and recording which can develop from it. Continuity in learning will be supported if adults are aware of the threads of learning – which will promote mathematical thinking throughout life.

4

Implementing a curriculum for mathematical thinking

In this chapter the focus will be the approaches which adults take towards the teaching and learning of mathematics. The elements of successful learning have been considered; as have the content and processes which must be learnt if children are to develop mathematically in a satisfactory way and are to become effective mathematical thinkers. As children grow and develop from birth onwards, the ways in which they interact with others, play and make choices will change but they will not disappear. As they experience more the need for the physical and playful ways of knowing will be complemented by other thinking processes, but will not be wholly replaced. They will remain important, not just throughout childhood but throughout life.

The chapter will focus on the kinds of provision that should be made to support learning in this area of the curriculum and the principles which need to underpin the experiences and activities which children are engaged in. The principles cover five main aspects of provision and are as follows:

- There must be time and space for playfulness
- There should be opportunities for communication and social interaction – either before, after or during the activity or experience
- There should be opportunities for choice and flexibility
- Mathematics should be made relevant to children's real-life experiences of the world and/or to their concerns and interests

- Children should be supported in making connections between the new learning and established learning or experiences.

Table 4.1 identifies some of the ways in which links may be made between the content and learning curricula. The sections that follow first consider the principles in greater detail and then relate all seven areas of mathematical development to different age groups and the principles outlined above.

Playful mathematics

> *Child:* When I play with my friends we have lots of fun . . . do lots
> of things . . . think about stuff . . . and . . . well . . .
> *Adult:* Do you learn about anything?
> *Child:* Heaps and heaps – not like sums and books and things . . .
> um . . . like . . . well . . . like real things!
> (Moyles 1994; cover blurb to first edition of *The Excellence of Play*)

Playful approaches to mathematics are essential for a number of reasons. Humour is fundamental to children's learning from infancy (Trevarthen 1998). Play (as discussed in Chapter 3) supports children in co-ordinating learning through a range of processes including practising, socializing, imagining and exploring. This section aims to go beyond the free-flow play which is so vital in supporting imagination and abstract thought and will include aspects of experience which are playful.

Child-initiated play

Mathematics as one way of the ways in which the world can be described will inevitably feature in children's play. Children will encounter mathematical elements as they work to discover more about the world around them and to make sense of it. This understanding, like other ways of describing the world, will not emerge naturally or magically but through the intervention of adults, which is discussed more fully in the next chapter. In schools and other settings for young children, it is vital not only that teaching focuses on preplanned activities such as cooking or the introduction of a new number rhyme but also that adults capitalize on responses that arise in children's play or self-initiated activity (QCA 2000). Not all self-initiated activity is play and not all playful activity is self-initiated. Griffiths (2005) puts forward five arguments for promoting mathematical learning through play. She says that play-based activity gives a purpose for learning, provides a concrete

Table 4.1 The relationship between content and the learning curricula

	Numbers	Calculating	Shape, space and measures
Guessing	Missing out numbers or making mistakes when counting out loud encourages children to challenge what they hear and feel braver about guessing. Encouraging children to guess the correct order when numbers on a number line have been misplaced	Sensible answers can only be arrived at if you first have an idea of what the answer might be. So encouraging children to always have a rough idea of the answer to any calculation is an excellent life-long strategy. 'I wonder how many more blocks you'll need to make all the walls as high as this one?'	Programmable toys (such as Bee-Bot, Roamer or Pixie) are great for encouraging guessing because you have to guess the sequence of movements required to get from one place to another. Using digital scales to check children's estimates of the weight of parcels
Identifying pattern	Songs, rhymes and stories which themselves have a pattern promote understanding of the pattern of numbers. Number squares make the patterns of numbers visible to children. Highlighting the patterns that children make in their in 2-D and 3-D work e.g. 'I see you've used two leaves and one petal in every corner.'	Identifying patterns in the week and calculating how many more apples or stories will be needed Looking for patterns in daily events, e.g. numbers of boys and girls away or present each day Adapt number rhymes, e.g 10 green bottles to explore pattern by for example taking two away each time	Blocks or small construction materials, e.g. Lego, can be used to encourage children to create patterns and to identify patterns in other children's work. Pattern Blocks are also an excellent resource for exploring pattern. Music, dance and movement enable children to explore patterns in space and time.

	Numbers	Calculating	Shape, space and measures
	Commenting on patterns in small world and imaginative play e.g. 'Oh look there are three animals in every field and one person in each car,' or 'Every doll at the table has one knife, one plate and two spoons.'		Describing patterns in the real world and analysing the components Use of mirrors and OHTs to explore pattern
Developing abstract thought	Promoting visualization by playing games with an array of objects covered and then children have to guess what has been taken away (or added?)	Placing a small number of objects in a container (e.g. box or bag); adding or subtracting some from the container and asking children how many are now in the container Using bun tins with a clear pattern when cooking gives children visual images to draw on – the patterns they provide promote visualization of number bonds Games which encourage visualization such as those using sets of beans or counters painted red on one side only; when children tip their five beans on to the table	Trying to decide what might fit/or could be inside an attractive selection of boxes or bags Gradually unfolding pieces of cloth or paper and asking children to think what the shape reminds them of and guess the shape which will emerge Giving children flattened boxes (or nets) to discuss what shape they might become; what might fit in them when made up

		they can instantly see the number bonds (3 red and 2 white; or 1 red and 4 white)	
Problem-finding	Investigating with a small number of cubes, pattern blocks etc., e.g. How many different ways can you arrange these five cubes? How many different ways can you arrange these six cars in the parking spaces? Finding boxes or bags which will hold only a particular number of things, e.g. This bag will hold only 4 cars; this bag will hold only 4 pegs etc.	A selection of trays that have held sweets, apples, eggs, ice cubes etc. and objects to fit in them. Discuss with children how many more of any one object will be needed to fill a particular tray.	Exploring collections – discuss similarities, differences, comparing materials, textures etc. A collection of balls for example would include problem-finding opportunities for seeing which would bounce best (and how this would be judged), which would roll furthest etc.

context for mathematics, allows children to take both control and responsibility, provides an opportunity for pressure-free practice, and is practical rather than written. All these things are useful, but to them should be added that it involves physical action, the basis of all learning.

However, many people would say (see, for example, Fisher 2002; Edgington 2004; Bruce 2005a) that much of the play which Griffiths is describing is not play at all but teacher-directed activity. Children need a balance of teacher-directed and self-initiated activity, which must include the time and space necessary to engage in what Bruce (1991) has termed 'free-flow play'. In many classrooms the balance is heavily tilted in the direction of teacher-initiated activities, and play is all too frequently relegated to something that happens when children have completed their work.

Moyles (1994: 3) records an observation of 7-year-old Wayne's activity in the class greengrocer's shop:

> He checks the till for money, counts each set of coins, recounts the single pennies (discovering only three) and rehangs the paper bags on the hook on the wall. He calls across the classroom for a customer . . . Wayne hands his customer a bag saying 'Good morning. This shop's self-service – you can 'ave wot you wants but you 'ave to pay me.' The customer duly takes a bag, fills it with apples and hands it to Wayne. 'Them's good for ya teeth,' he suggests, adding, '6p each, that's 24p . . . please madame. Can ya give me it right 'cos I ain't got much change today!'

This contrasts sharply with the 'planned play' activities outlined in the foundation stage pack produced by the National Numeracy Strategy (DfES 2002 Nursery Pack: 48). In the pack appear small group activities such as an adult drawing lines on a piece of paper for parking spaces for six toy cars. The questions to be asked are specified:

How many cars are parked?

How many if another car comes to park?

How many cars if one drives out?

How many parking spaces are there?

How many if we draw one more?

Such questions may have a place in teaching but they are far from playful. (It should also be noted that the same document fails to make a distinction between play and cooking. You can certainly play at cooking but cooking is not play.) Activities of this sort which share the resources of children's self-initiated and self-motivated play cannot take the place of play. They are adult-directed activities. There is a place for both kinds of activity but both are not genuine play. Only one type gives children control, exploration and the opportunity to refine and rehearse their understanding – in ways which will support the development of abstract thought. A balance needs to be maintained so that opportunities for children's free-flow play are not lost or diverted. The two kinds of activities fulfil very different purposes. Worthington and Carruthers (2003, citing Bostrom 1997) urge caution in using play in a shop to teach about giving change. If an adult uses a shopping expedition or a class shop to teach about change that is an adult-directed activity but when children are playing imaginatively at going shopping they are exploring aspects of change-giving in quite a different way. We might say that the 'penny drops' in a totally different way.

A conversation about buying and selling cars which takes place in the block area (Worthington and Carruthers 2003: 160-1) offers children the opportunity to explore complex ideas and begin to make sense of them and the adult an insight into children's understandings. Carl offers the teacher a car for £40 but when she suggests that that is too expensive he offers another for £50. However he subsequently offers her one for £10. One explanation for this shift in thinking may be that Carl detects his error in the unspoken reaction of the teacher; another may be that in speaking out loud Carl becomes aware of the flaws in his thinking. The point is that in a play situation there is no loss of face – children can explore ideas confidently and without fear of failure. The insight offered to the teacher enables her to plan other future experiences which will help Carl to reflect on ideas of cheaper and more expensive, greater and smaller.

Games

There are any number of commercially produced games which can be chosen to meet specific learning objectives. However, teachers should ensure that children also have access to familiar games and can choose to play them over and over again – in much the same way as they choose favourite books. At home, for example, 4-year-old David played a large and rather complicated board game designed for older children and adults. The family had enjoyed playing it together but David, on his own in every spare moment of the day for several weeks played by himself. He checked the rules or asked for explanations from adults and older siblings from time to time but in the main managed the game independently, acting as a number of players. The specific learning objectives would have been hard to identify but for him were undoubtedly connected to his determination to understand rule-based games. In the process, he practised one-to-one correspondence, counting on, identifying numbers on a dice, but these skills were not his aim.

Some teachers create their own games, to complement children's current interests or the class topic. Buck (1996) describes games made in the nursery school where she worked. They are linked to the school's emphasis on environmental education and designed to teach some complicated concepts. The mathematical learning in these games is incidental but none the less present in such features as using dice and developing strategic thinking. Similarly Gifford (2005b) describes a group of 4-year-old children working collaboratively to devise rules for a commercial game for which the instructions had been lost. She comments:

> I subsequently found the instructions which involved each child ordering a set of cards. Not only was the children's version at a more appropriate level, the innovative, collaborative element reduced the amount of turn-taking.

David's use of the game was self-initiated but usually games tend to be adult-directed. Lesley Hill (in Marsden and Woodbridge 2005: 19), describes a research project based on children's own games, using a simple blank game board (basically a 4 × 10 grid which allows children to move in parallel along the board from the start point to the finish:

> I wanted the children to devise their own game that I could observe and analyse, to see where to go next. The hardest part for me during the game was keeping quiet. I wanted to answer their questions, help them with their problems, protect them and be their teacher! Did I think they would learn more being directed by me? No, unfortunately, after analysing the transcripts, I found the adult-led games that we played when the game board was first introduced were shorter, less complicated and also less 'playful'. The children didn't have as many opportunities to explore and express their ideas, thoughts and feelings. Sometimes they didn't even have time to think, with adults busily pushing the game on for their own purposes.

The games the children devised in Hill's reception class drew on their existing knowledge of games but also led them to develop new rules. After her initial introduction of the idea of devising games, the children had a host of ideas. They incorporated imaginative ideas which increased their involvement, using for example dolphins and killer whales as part of a game in which getting a minus score sent you closer to the whale. As one child commented at the end of the game (Marsden and Woodbridge 2005: 39): 'It was sad when the mummy lost her two babies eaten by the killer whale.' They devised maze games and outdoor games, taught other children in the class to play their games and took them home to play with parents.

Books, songs, rhymes and stories

Books and stories offer playful exploration of mathematical ideas. Margaret Meek's (1982) assertion that we define reality by exploring unreality reminds practitioners that children learn from stories. Vivian Gussin Paley's (1981) curriculum in her American kindergarten was based on story. Children's discussions in her classroom allowed them to clarify their thinking and enabled her to gain insight into it. On one occasion the children have shared the story of 'Stone Soup' and decide to boil some stones to check out whether soup could be made in this way. After an initial hour long boiling, the children are sure that the stones are smaller. Further discussion ensues and they draw round them and boil them again. Because they remain unconvinced that the stones have not grown smaller, the teacher suggests weighing the stones. After more boiling, she suggests to them that the weight before and after is the same and that therefore the stones did not melt. But Eddie has the last word and finally adds that 'they only got a little bit smaller' (Paley 1981: 18). The language of the discussion is supported by physical action – acting out stories and boiling stones allow children to think with their bodies.

Songs and music support a playful atmosphere, promoting a sense of social cohesion (Pound and Harrison 2003) and supporting the rehearsal of mathematical ideas. As discussed in Chapter 3, songs make numbers memorable and thus promote counting. Helen MacGregor (1998) has used this function of music to support many other aspects of mathematical understanding. Using known tunes she has devised songs to support mathematical themes including two- and three-dimensional shape, calculation and pattern. Action rhymes, especially if they can be supported by props allow children to rehearse mathematical ideas playfully with physical action that reinforces learning and enjoyment. The props can be commercially bought toys, pictures (with magnetic strip or Velcro) or items made by children. Schiro (2004) emphasizes the use of props or what he terms 'manipulatives'. He likens them to 'magic objects' and suggests that they hold attention and promote involvement.

Figure 4.1 Counting books and small-world props to match

An additional advantage of props are that they enable children to retell or rehearse the stories or rhymes. Schiro (2004: vii) claims that while the use of children's literature to 'enrich mathematics instruction', oral retelling which 'abandons the written word and picture book' takes such learning and teaching to a higher level since it transforms the abstract, objective, deductive mathematics we all have experienced in school into a subject surrounded by imagination, myth and subjective meanings and feelings (Schiro 2004: viii).

Playful conversation

Many adults working with young children lack the confidence to make mathematical conversations playful. If a child offers a pretend sweet or refers to the lion under the chair, most adults familiar with working with young children tend to enter into the fun of the game. But if instead they claim that they have three cats or nine pencils, adults seem to want to put the mistake right. Gifford (2005b) comments on being the 'victim of a number joke' and highlights the value of this humour. She highlights the fact that in making these jokes, children are playing with or exploring the ideas, they are taking control of challenging material and coming to understand it better by taking it apart, and combining it in new ways. They are in short using their innate creativity to learn about the world.

Mathematical discussion, questioning and problem-solving can also be playful. Paley (1981: 186) describes a conversation with the class about giving change. The discussion continues over a period of several days. At some points the children agree that 'they're all the same quarters' but rapidly revert to worrying about which quarter they brought to school. The teacher herself brings a dollar to school and Eddie tells her to put her dollar in the jar, take out four quarters and put one back in – it is too big a step to put in a dollar and take out 75 cents.

Shakuntala Devi (1990: 9) describes her early love of numbers. She writes:

At three I fell in love with numbers. It was sheer ecstasy for me to do sums and get the right answers. Numbers were toys with which I could play . . . My interest grew with age. I took immense delight in working out huge problems mentally . . . there is a . . . richness to numbers: they come alive, cease to be symbols, . . . and lead the reader into a world of intellectual adventure where calculations are thrilling.

Few of us ever attain that degree of mathematical playfulness. However, Mertlens's (1996: 165) story shows that when children understand that thinking plays a role in their learning they can use play to good effect. She writes:

A small child stopped me with the words 'You're the maths person, aren't you?' I confessed to being such a one. He continued 'Do you want to know something? D'you know that if you start with two and you go right on doubling eventually you get to one thousand and twenty-four!' As he said this last number, he threw his arms wide to indicate the extent and the size of this magnificent number. I expressed a suitable admiration, and he told me in an offhand manner: 'I learned that in bed!'

Even the wonder with which young children tell us simple but amazing facts such as 'D'you know? One and two make three *and* two and one make three,' should remind us of the continuing need for playfulness and excitement. Gifford (2005b) refers to young children's 'spontaneous, recombination of elements, joy of mastery and glint in the eye joviality'. We should not forget that young children's exuberance (or what Egan 1988 calls their 'ecstatic responses') have an important function in learning. The excitement makes learning more effective – it means that children want to know more!

Social interaction

Social interaction is at the root of all learning. Human beings have a propensity to seek out human contact, and many of our earliest contacts with babies are designed to give them a way into communicating with other humans. Conversation – with adults and with our peers, in small and large groups – is indispensable to both understanding and to the development of mathematical thinking. As a rule of thumb, the younger the child, the smaller the group within which he or she can profitably interact. School improvement studies and Ofsted documents stress the efficiency of whole-class teaching. When working with young children this poses some problems. Whole-class teaching can only be efficient if the teacher can be certain that everyone is engaging with what is being said not just by him or her but by everyone.

As adults we are able to interact with the ideas presented by one person to a group of hundreds, but even for us our thoughts are sometimes diverted by things said with which we do not agree or which we do not understand. For little children, whose thinking is rarely internalized, their ideas, misunderstandings and connections need to surface and need to be shared. This is difficult to achieve in a large group. Anyone who has ever been responsible for a primary school assembly will empathize with Samantha's story. Samantha was new to the reception class and was sitting close to the front. The headteacher was reading a story to the assembled gathering, carefully chosen to meet the needs of the youngest children. At regular intervals Samantha tried a range of strategies to attract the head-teacher's attention. She pointed, she tapped the head's shoe, she called her name and (quick to learn about rules) she even tried raising her hand. Eventually the headteacher stopped the story and asked Samantha what it was she wanted to say. As Samantha announced, 'My nan's got a pink hat!' the older children collapsed into gales of laughter. It would be all too easy to interpret her behaviour as showing a lack of awareness, but it was quite the reverse. Struggling to make sense of what to her seemed incomprehensible, the child had spotted in the corner of one page a tiny figure wearing a pink hat. Until she had confirmed the link she was unable to focus on the story and was therefore anxious to communicate what was for her the only point of contact.

For over the past thirty years (Donaldson 1976) we have known that little children do not just make sense of what they hear but are constantly trying to interpret events, words and actions within a context. Large groups make it difficult for children to have sufficient interaction and to ask sufficient questions for them to make sense of what is going on. This is true for all young children but especially so for those in the early stages of learning English or who have comprehension difficulties. Although the learning needs of these two groups are very different, the strategies for supporting them are similar. Opportunities to communicate ideas with the support of adults and other children, visual materials which give children some additional clues about the topic under discussion and a group size which allows children sufficient time to contribute will all help.

Fisher (2002) reminds us that different groupings have different purposes. She identifies four purposes of whole-class sessions: telling children things, imparting knowledge to them, making them enthusiastic and sharing ideas. These are all vital so long as children are at a stage where they can recognize that what is being said is addressed to them. So often, little children switch off from large-group sessions – at home and in more intimate interactions they are used to being able to check their own understanding by asking questions, asking for things to be repeated and by contributing and sharing anecdotes which help them to relate what is being said to their own understanding. With all that has been said about the difficulties of the specialist use of language in mathematics and the emphasis which needs to be placed on thinking (which for little children is frequently spoken) it is plain that large-group sessions should be used sparingly. The danger signs of fidgeting, switching off or disruptive behaviour should be heeded – they should alert adults to the fact that the situation may no longer be productive. It may even, if children are learning that maths is boring or incomprehensible, be counterproductive.

None of this means that instruction is not an important element of teaching. Parents use instruction even with very young children, but it will only be effective in situations where children can either initiate the topic of instruction according to their interests or develop a passionate interest from the way in which they are introduced to new experiences and activities. It is this interactive approach which is vital in supporting young children's learning and development and it is precisely this which is difficult to achieve where staffing ratios are unfavourable. Young children need the sensitive support of adults as they strive to make sense of the world, including the world of mathematics. The continuum continues to be important: 5-year-olds do not need the same support as 5-month-olds, but needs do not simply disappear. Ball (1994) suggests that group sizes should be linked to the age of the child. Doubling the age of the child indicates the appropriate maximum grouping.

Sylva (1997: 20) underlines the importance of the need to maintain for under-5s 'an optimum balance between guided and self-initiated learning'. This must be achieved by recognizing that the optimum balance may be different for children of different ages, in different kinds of provision and at different stages in the dual development of dependency and interdependence. There must be genuine opportunities for children to develop the social and emotional competence necessary for them to work comfortably among their peers. Paley (1990) describes her efforts to create social networks among the children with whom she works as 'drawing invisible lines between the children's images'. She seeks to help them to connect their thoughts, to see things from the perspectives of others. The very common arguments in the play shop between 3-year-olds about whether it is the shopkeeper or the customer who pays, for example, give children new ideas to think about. Group interaction can also help children to become aware of other possibilities. The high expectations set for one child can spur another to greater efforts or challenge their thinking.

Social interaction allows for the sustained shared thinking which Siraj-Blatchford and her colleagues (2002) characterize as contributing to problem-solving, clarifying ideas or concepts, evaluating experiences and extending stories. Hill (in Marsden and Woodbridge 2005: 79) reflects on the opportunities for high quality thinking which the research into mathematical games offered; she comments that children 'are assisted by reflective and questioning adults and, of course, by all the other thinking children in the class'.

Choice and flexibility

Choice is important to young children's learning and development for many reasons. First, if they are to become independent thinkers they need to learn to make independent decisions, alongside the many occasions in group settings where children may not act independently and where they must successfully coexist within a larger group.

Second, their persistent concerns will not always readily conform to the central themes of the classroom or of each other. Ideas may spring up which should be allowed to be followed through – to be developed into areas of expertise. If we really respect the needs of young children to represent their ideas and translate them in a variety of ways then there will need to be opportunities for many choices. Young children, whose ability to wait and to maintain an unfulfilled idea is limited, will need to be able to choose between representing their ideas in, for example, role play, paint, blocks or music. They will need to learn to select from different coloured pens and papers when representing their ideas and feelings. They will need to decide whether Lego or Mobilo will most effectively recreate their chosen image. As their control and competence grow, teachers may limit choices in order to offer additional challenges, but for the youngest children the choices (and support to explore and make decisions) generally need to be wide. Children themselves often set limits and create manageable challenges for themselves. Lewis (1996: 17) describes a group of children undertaking an investigation. She writes:

> In an activity to find and record how many different ways five multilink could be fixed together, it was the younger children in the group who had better ideas for organising the task. They said things like, 'We won't do twists because there would be so many' or 'We'll only do shapes that can lie flat on the table.' They were setting the parameters for the investigation and also justifying every model as they went.

The third reason for emphasizing the importance of choice is related to the need for children to make connections in their learning. The nature of young children's learning is necessarily idiosyncratic. If you've only been alive for 18 or 36 or even 50 months you have little experience with which to connect. Each toddler's limited experience will have relatively few points of overlap with the experiences of other toddlers of a similar age. Their choices will reflect their own concerns and sometimes come to mirror the choices of others.

Flexibility is what we hope will develop in children, but it is also essential in adults. Regular observations of children's learning will provide adults with insights which they can assess against their priorities for the child. The curriculum map offered by documents like the National Curriculum and the early learning goals offer objectives against which children's progress may also be judged. Regular evaluation of children's records will enable staff to keep in mind what they want children to learn over time and seize on opportunities that arise in children's play and through discussions with them. This will be discussed further in the next chapter.

Children can develop flexible ideas through discussion – a choice of vocabulary or strategy may be introduced, sometimes in a planned way, sometimes by chance. The shared sustained thought gives children to a range of ideas. The following conversation (recorded by Hill, in Marsden and Woodbridge 2005: 40) about what thinking is illustrates the way in which children can build on one another's ideas:

Dylan: You think about it first, you speak it in your head and then you speak it out from your mouth: that's the important bit.

Katy: If I want to think it's in my brain.

Owen: You have to remember it.

Dylan: In your brain you remember it.

Katy: It gets there from when you listen, tells them what other people have said.

George: And when you talk that's thinking and telling.

Relevance

In order to be relevant to children the curriculum should have continuity from birth through all phases of education. The introduction of the foundation stage is improving continuity between nursery settings and there are also attempts to improve continuity between the foundation stage and Year 1 of Key Stage 1 (see for example London Borough of Lewisham nd). Although the importance of continuity at formal stages has been recognized, it is still important to give as much support as possible as children move from one childminder or key person to another, from one class to another.

Discontinuity can arise when teaching does not take sufficient account of what children already know. Continuity of learning is supported when practitioners acknowledge the role of the earliest aspects of learning in later mathematical learning. Relevance is likely to be very much dictated by each child's personal experience. This underlines the need for choice and for social interaction – these things together will make it possible for the curriculum to meet the needs of all. When giving examples or making analogies, adults need to make sure that a wide range is included so that everyone in the group can relate to what is being talked about. Relevance is also linked to pleasure for young children – we can make difficult things relevant – we just need constantly to remind ourselves how important it is to do so.

All children, for example, have some knowledge of numbers – although what they have may not neatly correspond to what the textbooks or schemes of work assume. One area of knowledge which they often have is an interest in big numbers – knowing, for example, that a million is a lot is exciting. Even toddlers know about 'only one more'. Hall *et al.* (1996: 49) detail a conversation between two children in a nursery class. One is using the telephone, both are enjoying big numbers:

Gail: Do you want a hundred apples?

Andrew: Yes.

Gail:	(into phone) Hiya. A hundred apples. (pause . . . to Andrew) A hundred oranges?
Andrew:	Yes.
Gail:	(into phone) A hundred oranges. (to Andrew) A hundred pears?
Andrew:	Yes.
Gail:	(into phone) A hundred pears please.

Sean, whose enjoyment of 99 million was described in Chapter 1, was fascinated by the differences between 90 and 9 million, 30 and 3 million, 10 and 1 million. He spent over an hour creating the numbers on a calculator, referring to an adult from time to time to check what he had done.

Throughout this book an emphasis has been placed on the importance of linking the more abstract forms of mathematics to children's first-hand experiences. For young children real-life experiences are important not just on this basis but as continued grist to their mill. Real-life experiences are needed to extend and develop their understanding of the world in general, which is of necessity very limited. A child of statutory school age has little more than 60 months of experience. Among those entering a reception class with a single point of entry, the oldest will have 60 months of experience, while the youngest will have only 80 per cent of that. Real-life experiences like riding on a bus, visiting the market and pegging out the washing offer children the opportunity to reflect on their own experience and to compare it to the experiences of other children. For younger children in day care, they provide a chance to learn from everyday experiences which they might otherwise miss out on. Such activities are rich in mathematical potential.

Cooking provides a commonly used example. In early years settings cooking is often cited as a useful mathematical activity, and of course it is. It may include counting, weight, estimation, capacity and volume. However, it also includes a wide range of possibilities which includes small motor control, scientific concepts, the opportunity to develop vocabulary, sharing, planning and sensory experience. It will only support mathematical thinking if adults actually develop and exploit the mathematical elements. If staff are focusing on number, for example, with a group of children then recipes that focus on number may be chosen to reinforce understanding. This can be achieved through recipes that use a specific number of spoonfuls, eggs, vegetables or fruits. A similar focus on weight or halving or area (How many biscuits can we cut from this piece of dough when we've rolled it out?) may be planned.

Relevance may also stem from the materials and resources we use. Of course, children will need time to explore new resources – see how they differ from or are similar to others they have seen. Information and Communications Technology (ICT) resources such as calculators, digital cameras and robots or programmable toys can be highly stimulating partly because they link with home and partly because they offer new mathematical challenges. Some computer software also has mathematical potential but staff need to ensure that children take the time needed to engage in physical activities which will enable them to 'build intelligent muscles' (Healy 1999). Computers need to supplement, not supplant physical engagement.

However, if early learning is to be effective, early childhood educators must not lose sight of the possibility that children have questions that go beyond 'how much' and 'how many'. Real-life experiences have meanings which both go beyond and encompass mathematics and the other subjects, disciplines or areas of experience.

We may identify possible learning outcomes, but we must be prepared for the fact that young children's interests may lead them into alternative paths. They will not always learn what we set out to teach them. We must constantly evaluate both what they have learned and what we hope to teach them. For example, some nursery school children had been taken to the Natural History Museum to follow up a project on mammals. On returning to school, they were asked what they had liked best. 'Going upstairs on the red bus,' said Matthew!

Children's own concerns (see Chapter 2) will also make learning situations relevant or otherwise to children. Their concerns may arise from:

- dominant schema, such as enveloping or transporting
- recent significant events such as the birth of a new baby, or a visit to the circus
- favourite songs and stories
- things with which they are currently emotionally engaged.

Katy's comment about the mother dolphin being sad that her two babies were eaten by the killer whale is an example of this kind of engagement.

Connecting learning

In their self-initiated play and activity, children follow up their own concerns and interests. This can sometimes be mistaken for lack of concentration: 'Children, who appear to be flitting from one activity to another, may in fact be exploring a particular idea or concept in some depth.' (Manning-Morton and Thorp 2001: section 8: 8)

If the organization of resources gives children the opportunity to select materials for themselves they will be able to explore persistent concerns more effectively. Since the arrival of her baby sister, Sandy's overwhelming interest was in mothers and babies. She searched for large and small versions of the same thing – even talking about mummy and baby blocks. Her interest stimulated the interest of other children and there were rich discussions about relative sizes and the relative nature of concepts of big and small.

Jake's interest in length led him to unravel and rewind string and wool from the workshop area. He found some till rolls and experimented with walking in a straight line as far as he could. He was introduced to the Bee-Bot robot and this was of interest to him because one press of the forwards (or backwards) button caused it to move its own length. Jake had great fun and developed expertise in learning to make accurate estimates of how many times he needed to press the button to make the toy move from one place to another.

One of the major ways in which adults can support children in making connections is in creating cross-curricular links. Table 4.2 indicates ways in which aspects of learning in other areas of the curriculum can support mathematical thinking and development. Additionally, a range of problem-solving activities and practical experiences such as cooking offer opportunities for learning across the curriculum including mathematics. Skinner (2005) makes a wide range of suggestions for maths trails. One of the suggestions she makes is a pattern walk, in which photographs of different patterns and textures, natural and manufactured, are taken and made into a book. Another suggestion is to create an obstacle course, in which children find a variety of ways to crawl or climb over, under, through and so on. Both of these suggestions offer clear opportunities for mathematical learning but also support learning in other areas of the curriculum – including physical development, creative development, knowledge and understanding of the world and communication, language and literacy.

Creative approaches to mathematics

In some Lewisham schools, work is being developed to find ways of making mathematics more accessible to young children. MakeBelieve Arts produced a series of theatre in education productions entitled 'Dramatic Mathematics'. The productions in schools were followed up by the production of a resource pack (Lee and Tompsett 2004) to support

Table 4.2 Relationship between early learning goals for mathematics and for other areas of learning and experience (based on QCA 2000)

Mathematical development	Communication, language and literacy	Creative development	Knowledge and understanding of the world	Personal, social and emotional development	Physical development
General support for mathematical development	Symbolization is a basic element of both linguistic and literary activity and of mathematics. Language for thinking is a key strand and will include mathematical thinking.	Aesthetic and creative activities (such as mathematics) are languages or representational systems which children may use as tools for thinking.	Exploration, investigating, identifying patterns and similarities and differences are all essential elements of mathematics.	A positive disposition to learning is the key to all successful learning. For too many people negative attitudes to mathematics get in the way of learning.	Physical action is the basis of all thought.
The development of guessing, pattern-finding and abstract thinking (Problem-solving/ finding is explored below.)	The development of language supports thinking – both in the abstract and in verbalizing ideas, predictions and hypotheses. As writing development, the process of symbolization described in the cell above supports the identification of mathematical patterns.	Pattern is a key element of music, story, poetry and visual arts. The process of imagining involved in the expressive arts supports the development of abstract thought.	Identifying patterns and similarities and differences are all essential elements of mathematics.	Confidence and a positive disposition to learning is the key to making use of the ability to predict, to identify and to articulate pattern. Creativity, like abstract thought, relies on imagination and risk-taking.	Physical action is the basis of all thought.

Number Say and use number names in order in familiar contexts. Count reliably up to 10 everyday objects. Recognise numerals 1–9.	Stories and rhymes that explore number (with props e.g. five speckled frogs) will support these goals. Counting books included in the book corner.	Getting children to help set up adult-directed activities or to describe the numbers of things they have used in their own paintings, drawings, musical improvisations etc.	Simple programmable toys require the use of small numbers – units forwards, backwards, numbers of turns etc. Exploring numbers in the environment e.g. house numbers, bus numbers.	Having the confidence to risk getting it wrong allows children to practise getting it right. Finding and focusing on numbers that are significant for children e.g. ages.	Clapping games and movements accompanying songs and music help children to understand number. Linking finger counting and numbers: the physical action reinforces the learning of the symbol.
Calculating In practical activities and discussion begin to use the vocabulary involved in addition, subtraction and comparing numbers. Begin to relate addition to combining two groups of objects and subtraction to 'taking away'. Find one more or less than a number from 1 to 10.	Stories and rhymes do this very well e.g. *The Doorbell Rang* by Pat Hutchins (1986).		Comparisons when shopping or collecting natural materials in the park. Cooking offers many such opportunities.	Sharing and turn-taking.	

Table 4.2 (*continued*)

Mathematical development	Communication, language and literacy	Creative development	Knowledge and understanding of the world	Personal, social and emotional development	Physical development
Shape, space and measures Use words such as 'greater', 'smaller', 'heavier' or 'lighter' to compare quantities. Talk about, recognize and recreating simple patterns. Use words such as 'circle' or 'bigger' to describe the shape and size of solid and flat shapes. Use everyday words to describe position.	A wide range of favourite stories explore these aspects of mathematics.	Use of malleable materials e.g. clay and dough enable children to explore quantity, area, size etc. Songs and music support exploration of pattern, space, shape and comparative language.	Exploring time and place. Looking closely at similarities, differences, patterns and change. Finding out why things happen and how they work – cause and effect. Building and constructing. Programmable toys.	Confidence is key to being willing to explore space.	Awareness of space in dance and other movement e.g. climbing, jumping etc. Travelling over, under, through etc.
Problem-solving Use developing mathematical ideas (about numbers and counting) and methods to solve practical problems.	Using graphics to think things through. Using language to imagine. Using talk to organise, sequence and clarify thinking.	Exploring and investigating texture, sound, colour, shape, form etc. Expressing and communicating ideas using a range of creative media.	The experience built up in a range of scientific, technological and geographical activities will provide an excellent foundation for problem-solving.	Confidence to try things out and risk getting it wrong! Working and negotiating with others in order to find solutions.	Physical solutions to problems – moving objects around supports later more abstract solutions.

Use developing mathematical ideas (about calculating) and methods to solve practical problems.	Drawing on the strategies identified in stories.
Use developing mathematical ideas (about shape, space and measures) and methods to solve practical problems.	

teachers of children at Key Stage 1 in extending and developing the mathematical ideas. The work has been based on the work of Egan (1989) who has hypothesized that teaching and learning across the curriculum (including mathematics) can be improved by being based on story.

The success of 'Dramatic Mathematics' coupled with current debates about the value of exploiting and developing creativity across the curriculum (DfES 2003) led MakeBelieve Arts to explore the potential of creative media in the teaching of mathematics. Their approach is based on the following tenets:

- Using the imagination to explore unreality and the unknown supports mathematical thinking by promoting abstract thought (Meek 1985; Paley 1990; Mazur 2003; Jenkinson 2001; Devlin 2000).
- Narrative supports learning in the early years (Egan 1988; Paley 1990).
- Narrative can support mathematical learning throughout the primary years (Devlin 2000; Schiro 2004; Whitin and Wilde 1995).
- Symbolic representation in a variety of modes supports thinking across all intelligences including mathematical intelligences (Gardner 1999; Malaguzzi 1995; Rogoff 2003; Egan 1988).
- There is increased understanding of the role of emotions (Goleman 1996; Gerhardt 2004) and of physical action (Bresler 2004; Doherty and Bailey 2003) in learning across the curriculum, including mathematics.

A project entitled Creative Approaches to Mathematics, funded by the Esmee Fairbairn Foundation has been piloted and is being developed further in Lewisham primary schools from the foundation stage through to year 4. The project is exploring ways of promoting mathematical understanding through the use of story, drama, music and visual arts.

Mathematics from 0 to 3

An under-threes curriculum must consider everything that the child experiences in the setting, all the interactions between the adults and the children and what the child encounters in the environment as well as the activities they are offered. Children do not see some parts of the day, or some activities, as being more important than others. All experiences are opportunities for experimenting, finding out, communicating and relating to others.

(Manning-Morton and Thorp 2001)

Throughout these years, children's development depends heavily on their interactions with adults who know them well enough to interpret their intentions. (If babies and toddlers are cared for outside the home at any point during the week, there will need to be close partnership between the parents and carers to ensure that their intentions are understood.) We are now also increasingly aware of how they benefit from interaction and contact with other children of all ages, including those close to them in age (Dunn 1988). Their focus is inevitably on making sense of their world and daily routines offer golden opportunities to help and guide them in this process.

Adults also have a vital role in modelling talk and play. Children's own play (whether solitary or alongside other children) should not be under-valued, for it is here that they are practising, rehearsing and representing things that they have seen, heard and experienced. It is here that they are laying the foundations for thought – including mathematical thinking. However, adults can nurture this early play by playing with children in order to model the process of making one thing stand for another, pretending, sequencing and exploring. Adults also have a vital role to play in helping children to sustain play by maintaining their interest. Once again the importance of building on the child's own interests is underlined – how often have you seen a toddler slide away from something he had been happily engaged in when an adult moves in and asks questions? The most effective support is watchful and sensitive to what the baby wants to do, supporting rather than diverting or distracting play.

Whatever the experiences offered to young children in these crucial years, the quality of care and stimulation they experience shapes their learning opportunities and forms the basis of all future learning. The curriculum of the subsequent years of early childhood does not supplant this foundation but should be seamlessly moulded to it. The curriculum should form a continuum which will encompass the notions of:

- building on children's own interests
- adults interacting with children's learning
- the need for play
- social interaction.

Routine tasks and day-to-day activities are used to help children learn about their world and their response to it. Good-quality provision will ensure that stimulation, fun and interaction are offered within a predictable order to the day, providing a clear rhythm.

Anything and everything within the environment will be seen as play materials by children of this age, so adults have to make sure that everything within reach is safe, neither harming the child nor, if precious, susceptible to damage. Heuristic play materials developed from an idea of Goldschmied (1990) offer babies and toddlers opportunities to explore and develop their sensory understanding – which will be the basis of future conceptual development. Throughout these years solitary and parallel play will be a dominant feature of their activity and this should be both respected and catered for – little children cannot happily wait for their turn. Learning to take turns will receive a greater focus later in their development. In group settings this will often mean having several of the same toys so that the current favourite can be enjoyed by more than one child.

From their earliest months babies can enjoy books and this has been recognized in the Book Start schemes (http://www.surestart.gov.uk/surestartservices/childcare/bookstart/) around the country to introduce babies to books at an early age. The repetitive language, striking illustrations and a cosy lap make books for young children an enjoyable and stimulating experience. Just as the adult's prime intention in sharing books with babies is not to teach them to read, so sharing number rhymes and joining in lively games is not solely about mathematical development. The enjoyment of learning and broadening horizons in general are among the adult's foremost but often unspoken intentions.

Compare this happy scene of books, rhymes, exploration, play and physical interaction with the picture summoned up by the work of Doman and Doman (1994). Their book sets out a method by which they claim very young children can be taught to recognize large numbers of spots drawn on big cards and to undertake some quite complex sums, including equations. If their claims are true, one is left asking why; although, to be fair, they do say that if either the parent or the child is not having fun then the work should be abandoned. The same concerns about linking the abstract nature of the symbols used to children's practical understanding will apply to these babies and toddlers as apply to children in the reception class being introduced to formal mathematics for the first time. Earlier does not necessarily mean better! What is perhaps of most concern about their work is that it violates the balance of adult-directed and child-initiated activity. They recommend, for example, that parents might put their mathematics programme (which requires three short practice sessions a day) into practice from birth. With a heavy emphasis on instruction, this leaves little time for play, interaction and exploration.

Table 4.3 shows links between mathematical development and the aspects of learning highlighted in the curriculum framework for children up to the age of three, *Birth to Three Matters* (Sure Start Unit 2002).

Table 4.3 Aspects of learning (identified in *Birth to Three Matters*, Sure Start Unit 2002) and mathematical development

A strong child	*Relevance to mathematical thinking and development*	*A competent learner*	*Relevance to mathematical thinking and development*
Me, myself and I (Realization of own individuality) Growing awareness of self Realizing one is separate and different from others Recognizing personal characteristics and preferences Finding out what one can do	These aspects of development are crucial to having the confidence to guess, the drive to seek out and solve problems and the sense of self that supports all learning and development (Siegel 1999).	**Making connections (connecting ideas and understanding the world)** Making connections through the senses and movement Finding out about the environment and other people Becoming playfully engaged and involved Making patterns, comparing, categorizing and classifying	Learning is all about connecting ideas – using sensory and other experience. Playing leads to abstract thought. Identifying patterns and categorizing are essential elements of mathematical development.
Being acknowledged and affirmed (experiencing and seeking closeness) Needing recognition, acceptance and comfort Being able to contribute to secure relationships Understanding that one can be valued and important to someone Exploring emotional boundaries	All of these aspects support mathematical development in that they enable the child to be in touch with other people's thinking and ideas (Siegel 1999).	**Being imaginative (responding to the world imaginatively)** Imitating, mirroring, moving, imagining Exploring and re-enacting Playing imaginatively with materials, using all the senses Pretend play with gestures and actions, feelings and relationships, ideas and words	Imaginative play, learning from what others model, learning to use and create symbols are all essential elements of mathematical development.

Table 4.3 (*continued*)

A strong child	Relevance to mathematical thinking and development	A competent learner	Relevance to mathematical thinking and development
Developing self-assurance (becoming able to trust and rely on own abilities) Gaining self-assurance though a close relationship Becoming confident in what one can do Valuing and appreciating one's own abilities Feeling self-assured and supported	Confidence is the key to guessing and to being able to stick with and follow up one's own original ideas.	**Being creative (responding to the world creatively)** Exploring and discovering Experimenting with sound, other media and movement Developing competence and creativity Being resourceful	Creativity and mathematics are not always thought of in the same sentence but mathematical thinking can and should be creative.
A sense of belonging (acquiring social confidence and competence) Being able to snuggle in Enjoying being with familiar and trusted others Valuing individuality and contributions of self and others Having a role and identity within a group	These aspects of learning underpin the confidence that children need to communicate and discuss with others.	**Representing (responding to the world with marks and symbols)** Exploring, experimenting and playing Discovering that one thing can stand for another Creating and experimenting with one's own symbols and marks Recognizing that others may use marks differently	These aspects of learning are laying the foundations for symbolic thought and behaviour – a vital aspect of mathematical thought and development.

Cameo: Ali's key person, Deb, knew that Ali enjoyed opening and closing doors, boxes, bags and so on. She collected together a dozen different small purses with different shapes, sizes and fastenings. Some had zip fasteners, some had Velcro strips, press studs, catches that had to be squeezed. One or two of the purses had more than one fastener. Inside each purse was a small object – a tiny car, a shell, a small stone and so on. Deb suggested to Ali that she needed to check that every purse had something in it. Ali was in her element. She loved the purses, delighted in finding the small objects and was particularly fascinated by a tiny purse constructed from three pieces of plastic which could only be opened by squeezing the pointed ends – which made a gap in the one unstitched side of the purse.

- **What was the mathematical learning?** Ali was learning about one to one correspondence, about size, shape, comparison. As Deb talked to her about the purses and as she later talked to her father about it when he came to collect her, Ali was developing mathematical vocabulary and learning to communicate and think mathematically. She was guessing about what might be inside each purse, she was problem-finding and solving as she attempted to find how each fastener worked. The task of putting the small items back into appropriate purses was also a problem-solving challenge. Pattern existed in the fact that each purse contained one item, with the exception of one which had two objects. This deviation from the pattern drew attention to the pattern. Finally Ali was learning to think in the abstract both by playing imaginatively with the items she found and by thinking about objects that could not be seen.
- **How did the provision support mathematical thinking and development?** The provision that Deb made was playful. Her engagement with Ali as she explored the purses made it a social and communicative experience. There was choice and flexibility in that Ali decided if and how she wanted to engage with the purses. The materials were relevant because they were based on Deb's observations of Ali's interests – and as such they also connected learning for her.

Mathematics from 3 to 5

The traditional activities found in nursery schools and classes, day nurseries and playgroups have been developed over many years to stimulate children's curiosity, to heighten their motivation to extend their learning beyond the routine tasks and materials of the home, and to support their desire to understand the world around them.

The need for a safe and predictable environment essential to the development of children up to the age of 3 remains but the balance needs to shift to include more new and shared experiences. Even familiar activities such as going shopping take on a new slant and offer a renewed learning opportunity – children are learning to see things with new eyes, to compare their experiences and to challenge one another's understandings.

The introduction of the early learning goals (QCA 2000) led some practitioners to place too much emphasis on adult-directed mathematical activities. It has also led many to plan only for mathematics indoors at the mathematics table. This is not what is required but is perhaps due to many practitioners' lack of confidence. In fact the *Curriculum Guidance for the Foundation Stage* (QCA 2000) requires that teaching should take place indoors and out, make use of the local environment, be cross-curricular, involve a balance of play and adult–directed activity and allow the necessary time and space for effective learning. This echoes Margaret McMillan's (1930) emphasis on allowing plenty of time and space in order to enable children to develop their understanding of themselves, others and the world.

A range of publications (Montague-Smith 2002; Skinner 2005; BEAM 2003) identify opportunities for learning mathematics in early years settings that are open-ended and may give teachers and other workers good ideas for developing the mathematics curriculum in all areas of provision, in both child-initiated and adult-directed activities. They underline the fact that mathematics can be taught and learnt in:

- Daily routines including circle time, story groups or snack times
- The outdoor area and the local environment
- All areas of provision, indoors and out – role play, mark-making, music and dance and so on
- All areas of learning – through activities planned to promote physical or creative development for example
- Child-initiated experience in continuous and enhanced provision (Marsden and Woodbridge 2005) as well as adult-led activity.

This is helpful in encouraging confidence among staff as to what constitutes mathematics. Even those staff most lacking in confidence can, as they collect observations of children's responses in these kinds of activities, begin to gain insight into the breadth and depth of children's mathematical understanding.

Much less helpful are those publications which produce series of worksheets for use in nursery classes. Worthington and Carruthers (2003: 6) conducted a survey about the use of worksheets. The study involved 273 teachers and their results show that in primary schools all the classes used worksheets apart from reception classes, in which 11% of classes did not. Within provision for under-5s maintained nursery classes only 20% used them. Perhaps surprisingly, private nurseries demonstrated less use of worksheets (63%) than voluntary pre-schools where 72% of providers regularly used worksheets. As Worthington and Carrington (2003: 28, citing Cullen and St George 1996) comment: 'When teachers over-emphasise teacher directed tasks such as worksheets, children view learning as dependent on the teacher.'

There is no place in the nursery for worksheets. Fisher (2002) has identified some important principles to bring to mind when tempted to make use of worksheets. She reminds practitioners that worksheets do not give an accurate view of what children can do – only careful observation of what they do and say can give that insight. She underlines the fact that young children need to develop their own ways of recording their ideas. Finally, she advises teachers to think of more effective ways to address independence and self-initiated activity – worksheets are frequently used to keep children busy and seated in one place. Since the vast majority of children who have nursery places in Britain are in part-time provision, they have little enough time to play, explore and interact in group settings. Adults must not squander children's precious time by filling it with time-wasting time-fillers.

Cameo: Sam, the teacher in an early years unit introduced a large collection of balls. The collection included different kinds of sports balls, but also marble, cane, plastic, flashing, musical, carved wooden and even balls of wool and string. There was an interactive display but in addition balls were added to a range of areas within the classroom and the outside area. The sheer variety of the collection fascinated the children and interest was sustained over a huge range of experiences. Sometimes Sam introduced specific activities such as ordering the balls according to weight but more often he built on or enhanced ideas that the children developed. For example, when a group demonstrated excitement about rolling balls down the slide, the staff planned to give time and space to an investigation.

- **What was the mathematical learning?** Children had opportunities to learn about counting – the number and variety of balls invited this. So often we only give children small numbers of objects – but in fact they enjoy large quantities, in the same way as they enjoy big numbers. The ways in which the balls could be categorized encouraged calculation – were there more wooden or more plastic balls? Which ones could roll (or bounce) in a straight line and which curved? These resources offered almost unlimited opportunities for exploring shape, space and measures. In terms of the learning or process curriculum pattern, problem-finding and solving and guessing readily became part of conversations and experiences involving the balls. The staff planned to promote abstract thought by setting up some activities in which children were invited to fit balls of different sizes into different sized boxes and/or to guess which balls were inside which boxes.

- **How did the provision support mathematical thinking and development**? The provision was very playful – a spikey, floppy, green plastic ball, for example, could be squeezed into many different textures and shapes and was the source of great excitement. A tiny ball made from bent wicker and no bigger than a marble was matched by a similar one with a diameter of around 25 centimetres and again this delighted the children. The excitement generated communication at many different levels and invited a shared interest. The balls offered many choices and could be used very flexibly – and were highly relevant to children's interest and stage of development. The variety meant that children could engage with them in ways that were relevant to them. Some played ball games, some enjoyed the variety of patterns carved, painted or woven into the balls. The fact that the balls could contribute to every aspect and area of learning meant that connections were inevitably made.

Mathematics in the primary school

Increasing understanding of the need for continuity at points of transition makes it advisable to maintain the approaches which are being developed in the foundation stage. Where classes are large and staffing ratios unfavourable this may be difficult but the principles which underpin effective mathematical learning for children in nursery and reception classes continue to be important. Too often children are still directed to work through the materials at their own pace, regardless of their understanding. This inflexible practice, common in primary classes, of moving groups of children through the same activity is commented on by Clemson and Clemson (1994: 19):

> There is no theoretical justification for processing children at different rates through the same material. Rather, depending on the interests and desires of the child, a wide range of mathematical ideas should be available to children, and in a variety of classroom created contexts.

Worthington and Carruthers (2003) suggest that this approach reflects a world-wide trend to make increased use of commercial schemes for teaching mathematics. While teaching still too often relies on pre-structured schemes of work with insufficient differentiation, the National Numeracy Strategy (DfEE 1999) has gone some way to making teaching more varied. Although most children still have too many worksheets, the focus on oral mathematics and on children developing their own written methods has widened the range of activities and experiences provided for children at Key Stage 1.

There has also been some renewed use of structured materials developed in the 1950s and 1960s, such as Stern apparatus and Cuisenaire rods. A study reported by Tacon and Atkinson (1997) suggests that structured apparatus can help children to create mental images and thus support their ability to solve mathematical problems mentally. It should be supplemented by ready access to numberlines and number squares. Just as classrooms have alphabets, readily available for reference, so hundred squares, displayed so that children can refer to them, stimulate many children's interest.

Primary National Strategy

The National Numeracy Strategy (DfEE 1999) has some strengths as discussed above. The unvarying, timed structure has, however, some worrying aspects. Too often reception classes are expected to inflexibly conform to the structure. Perhaps even more worrying is that the structure has been adopted for other areas of the curriculum so that, for example, science and art are being too often taught in the same tight structure, undermining children's independence and constraining the amounts of time and space available to them. The other worrying aspect is the emphasis on pace. Pace is widely regarded as being a desirable aspect of a lesson. While it is absolutely true that pace contributes to effective class management. However as Claxton (1997) reminds us that quick responses are not always considered responses and we should at times be giving children time to explore what he terms the 'slow ways of knowing'. Despite these reservations, overall the focus on exploring and developing children's own mathematical insights is to be welcomed.

The introduction of the Primary National Strategy, following the publication of *Excellence and Enjoyment* (DfES 2003), is designed to encourage teachers to develop more cross-curricular approaches to literacy and numeracy. There are some signs that teachers are seeking ways to make mathematical learning at Key Stage 1 more playful and enjoyable. Tucker (2005) for example identifies a range of role play activities for children in Years 1 and 2.

Cameo: A group of children had become very interested in a book entitled *One is a Snail, Ten is a Crab* (Sayre and Sayre 2004). It is subtitled

A counting by feet book and as the title suggests one is a snail. Two is a person, four is a dog, six is an insect, eight is a spider and ten is a crab. (The authors assure the reader that the two claws serve a dual purpose as feet.) Odd numbers are constructed by adding a snail, for example, three is a person and a snail. Numbers beyond ten are made up in a variety of ways and the book goes up to 100 which is shown as being made up of ten crabs or 100 snails. A whole range of activities was based on this book – mobiles, investigations, imaginary animals and so on. Work was also developed from *Centipede's 100 Shoes* (Ross 2003) and linked to Helen MacGregor's (1998) song about centipedes and millipedes – which promotes counting backwards and forwards in tens and in hundreds.

- **What was the mathematical learning?** Children explored counting in tens forwards and backwards and also developed interest in counting in twos, threes, fours and so on. The fun and humour of the book encourages children to develop mental images of the different ways of making up numbers and to guess or predict different ways of making up numbers. The book offers a clear pattern and children were able to play with the ideas and create other patterns – using vehicles (unicycle, bike, trike, car etc.). Problem-solving is inherent in the structure of the text.
- **How did the provision support mathematical thinking and development?** It was playful and lively. It involved a great deal of communication and sustained shared thinking. The problem-solving element ensures some flexibility. The children's enthusiasm makes the material highly relevant. Learning is connected by extending the idea across the curriculum.

Summary

Adults offering children a curriculum to develop their mathematical thinking need to provide choices so that children can build upon their persistent concerns. They need to ensure that children interact with others – sometimes and for relatively short periods in larger groups but most effectively in small groups. Interaction with adults is vital, but learning also occurs in situations where children are interacting with their peers. The curriculum should reflect and build upon children's real-life experiences. Above all, it should offer time and space for playful approaches to mathematical learning, which will include teacher-directed activity. This cannot replace self-initiated play, but may, through games, books, stories and discussions, offer a variety of learning opportunities.

From birth to age 3, children's learning will be best supported by an emphasis on learning and developing through everyday experiences and routines. The traditional provision of group settings for older children offers the kinds of activity which allow children to think in action, representing their growing understanding of mathematics in play, talk, movement and sound, as well as two- and three-dimensional images. The early learning goals and National Numeracy Strategy exert pressures which practitioners who lack confidence sometimes interpret as unhelpful requirements. These should be judged in the light of all that is known about young children's learning and in that way can provide a helpful map of children's mathematical journey – to be safely stored in the practitioner's head.

5

Observing, planning and supporting mathematical thinking and learning

Extraordinary as it may appear, especially to those who believe strongly in the power of nurturing and who reject the notion that human beings are nothing more than a collection of genes, babies' prime carers generally have innate or natural knowledge of how best to support the development of their precious responsibility. In reality, just as the baby has a propensity to work at making sense of the world, to figure out the rules and to seek out human interaction, so others, including even slightly older children, have a propensity to do the things that will make that possible. Research (Papousek and Papousek 1987; Trevarthen 1990) shows us that the responses of adults to very young children are too rapid to have been consciously planned and must therefore rest on implicit understandings. Where, in research settings, the carer's responses are manipulated (through the use of video and mirrors) to be delayed or not matched to the actions of the baby, the latter shows real distress. In real-life rather than research settings, such delays may occur where the adult is not tuned in to the baby's needs. This may be because the adult is overwhelmed by pressures, possibly financial or emotional or both. It may be because his or her own experience of care as an infant is such as to evoke destructive memories which act as a barrier to good interaction with the baby. However, this is relatively rare and in general we must conclude that adults dealing with young babies in apparently unstructured settings, such as informal play in the home, do closely *observe* what their babies do and *intervene* appropriately.

The work of Wells (1985), for example, shows that in talking to their children, parents limit or structure the sentence complexity which they use to reflect children's understanding. They extend the complexity in two ways. If an adult uses a more complex structure by mistake and realizes that the child can cope with it, that will become part of the future repertoire when interacting with the child. Sentences with more than one clause are a common example of where this happens. Unusual words to which the child unexpectedly responds are another. Furthermore, if the parent hears the child use or respond to a more complex form they will again weave that into their conversations. A common example occurs in the use of 'I' and 'me'. Before children fully understand the importance of these words, adults get into very convoluted discussions with young children. Once they hear the child using them appropriately the trans-lations which accompanied earlier conversations such as 'Give it to me, give it to mummy' become redundant. Tremendously skilful and unconsciously reflective as this process is, it works well in the home where adults are generally dealing with just one baby who is very well known to them. Overt planning is unnecessary since the adults' prime goal is simply to bring the child successfully into the world of the family – which is modelled before the child every single day.

Within institutional care, adults will generally be dealing with larger numbers of children from a range of homes and cultures whose family values and customs will differ. The adults' role is to bring the children up not only according to the will of their family but also in line with the demands of society. Again there will usually be some common threads, but there will also be differences. Professional carers will have less inti-mate knowledge of the children's understandings and enthusiasms and their own goals for the children will be less focused because of conflicting demands. Thus professionals can rarely act in the same 'natural' way as parents. Observing and intervening remain crucial ingredients of the success of their work with babies and young children, but to these must be added planning. Careful planning will allow parents or other principal carers to discuss with staff what their child's experiences will be. Quality assurance procedures can be used to ensure that plans do not conflict with either families' concerns or children's entitlement. Without the involvement of all parties, observation will be based on restricted infor-mation and intervention may be based on a false premise.

Observing children's mathematical learning and thinking

Everyday things hold wonderful secrets for those who know how to observe and to tell about them.

(Gianni Rodari)

One of the exciting features of early childhood education is the way in which the pioneers or founders of the tradition – including such notables as Friedrich Froebel, Maria Montessori, Margaret McMillan and Susan Isaacs – were able to tease out the learning needs of young children through their own sensitive observation. Their insights (and the importance of a developmentally appropriate curriculum) are today increasingly supported by the findings of developmental psychologists and educationalists. In relation to the importance of social contact and emotional well-being (Vygotsky 1986, Siegel 1999; Gerhardt 2004), the role of movement in development (Athey 1990; Bresler 2004) and the benefits of developing both left and right functions of the brain (Claxton 1997; Greenfield 1996), the importance of the observations of the early pioneers is underlined. The terminology may have changed, but the messages are similar.

The stories that observations tell

In Reggio Emilia, adults working with young children in the city's nurseries understand that their observations of children's learning are of fundamental importance. The detailed notes (called 'documentation') kept by practitioners are used to help staff to develop a story or theory and thus to promote understanding of children's learning. Malaguzzi (1997: 11) writes:

> Though documentation may have originated as a way to offer children an opportunity to evaluate their own work and to keep parents better informed about school experiences, it was soon discovered to be an extraordinary opportunity for teachers to revisit and re-examine their own work with children, offering unquestionable benefits in terms of professional development . . . In this light, documentation becomes an integral part of educational planning and organisation and an indispensable tool for listening, observing and evaluating . . . it is my deep conviction that the world of school must begin to understand that producing documents and testimonies to the educational experience means drawing closer to a better understanding of the workings of the human mind and of children's learning styles and strategies of behaviour.

Vivian Gussin Paley also emphasizes the importance of narrative observations in understanding children's learning. In her book entitled *The Boy Who Would Be a Helicopter* (1990: xii) she writes about Jason and about teachers making sense of the world of learning:

None of us are to be found in sets of tasks or lists of attributes; we can be known only in the unfolding of our unique stories within the context of everyday events. We will listen to Jason's helicopter stories and offer our own in exchange . . . The story of Jason and his helicopter reminds us that every child enters the classroom in a vehicle propelled by that child alone, at a particular pace and for a particular purpose.

Evaluating the curriculum

Regular evaluation of children's ongoing records is essential. It ensures that the potential offered by areas of the nursery or classroom for developing mathematical thinking is recognized and that the emerging needs of young learners are regularly addressed. The observations of those who work with young children have stories to tell, not only about individual development, or about human learning in general, but also about the quality and relevance of provision. Practitioners' observations can tell them a great deal about the effectiveness of what they are planning and of what they have provided for children. If areas of provision are underused, or sometimes misused, practitioners should ask themselves whether that is because curriculum planning has been insufficiently thoughtful or reactive to children's needs. If a number of children are having difficulty with a particular area of development, is it because there has been insufficient opportunity for them to engage with relevant activities and learning experiences?

A nursery team, piloting a new assessment schedule for a publisher, was surprised to find that most of the children in the class were apparently unable to sort objects by length. This was an area that they had assumed the rich provision in the nursery made children aware of. They began to observe children engaged in activities where length was a potential topic of conversation. By discussing their observations, staff realized that provision did not routinely encourage children to consider length. Over time they began to make changes. In the outside water area they added piping of all lengths – some very short, some very long. In the creative workshop area they added a large number of very long and very short cardboard tubes. Into the dressing-up clothes were placed long pieces of ribbon and material. Long and short straws were placed on the milk table. Making banana bread provided an opportunity to discuss the relative lengths of the fruit and whether to use the longer or shorter baking tins. Conversations about longer and shorter cooking times promoted further thought. Ongoing observations showed that the children, after just a week or two, were more aware of length and comparisons and used the relevant vocabulary more frequently in their informal conversations.

Evaluation should include consideration of the extent to which equality of opportunity is being maintained within the setting. Evaluation of this type goes beyond looking at individuals and should seek to analyse what has been observed in the light of the response of *groups* of children. If no boys have chosen to go to the graphics area of the classroom, or if girls have not managed to use a computer all week, that is not only an issue about individual children but also a question of provision and intervention.

Observing the learning of individual children

Besides these broader purposes for observation lies the fundamental one of observing the learning of individual children. If we are really to see children operating at their most effective, the more natural and real the context in which we observe them the better. Just as we know that children's talk (and writing) is richer and more communicative when they have real things that are important to them to discuss, so it is with mathematics. Since play offers wonderful opportunities for observing what children can do, a classroom organised to support child-initiated activity will be helpful in making accurate assessments of children's learning. For young children, real mathematics will involve real-life activities, play and investigations. Games, especially where an adult is closely involved can give great insight into the development of individual children (Marsden and Woodbridge 2005).

If we make time to talk to children, to observe from a distance and to participate in their activity, we will gain a range of invaluable insights. Working with young children is so demanding that adults frequently find it difficult to stand back and watch. They may often feel that they are diverted from what they plan to do by a bleeding knee or a distressed arrival. Careful planning to ensure that all adults in the team have a clear agenda can help to ensure that vital observations are made.

There are issues about when and how to observe. These should be resolved through team discussion – decisions will be based on previous observations and staff evaluation. Written plans should identify children and areas to be observed. In order to assess young children's mathematical thinking, observations will need to draw on children's physical activity and their conversations. There is absolutely no issue about *who* should observe – all who are involved with and concerned for the child, including his or her parents and other principal carers, should be encouraged to contribute their unique perspective of the child's mathematical development. There is added strength in the differing viewpoints that adults bring to the way in which they observe, which will be derived from their training and experiences.

In relation to *what* to observe it is important that we do not simply observe activities that look 'mathematical'. In too many settings for young children, planning sheets have a box marked 'maths' which each day is filled in with suggestions like 'number puzzles', 'threading beads' and 'pegboards'. Of course these activities have mathematical potential and by involving ourselves in them we may learn something of what children know about mathematics. However, listening to their talk while they are with friends on the climbing frame or riding bikes may tell us about their understanding of space and position. Davies (1995: 61) describes 3-year-old Nicola playing on an empty clothes rail in a department store. She writes:

> Nicola had established an activity around the bottom rail and one of the uprights, saying aloud this sequence to herself as she moved: under and over under and over under and over round and round and round and round.

Such an observation – an everyday occurrence – tells us, if we have eyes to see and ears to hear, that Nicola has understanding of pattern (both rhythmic and linguistic) and that she can match the language and physical action of position. The better we know her the more likely we are to be able to make further hypotheses about the significance of a single observation. Gathering observations about a child's thinking and understanding can only be done effectively over time. It may be useful to think of it as somewhat like the Victorian art of *découpage* where layer is added to layer of a picture until a three-dimensional effect emerges. So it is with our observations. One observation or conversation tells us something, two observations tell us more, perhaps confirming our original view, perhaps conflicting with it. As time goes on we gather a clearer and clearer view, but always with a big question mark over it. Practitioners' observational evidence should always pose new questions which may be followed up in further observations, changes in provision and direct support for groups and individuals.

Video of children's activity over a period; scrappy notes made hurriedly at the sand tray; audio-tapes of conversations at the dough table or musical patterns played on the piano; narrative observations following specific incidents or activities in which we have been involved; time or incident samples maintained throughout the day on specific children or specific actions; photographs and children's own recorded work – all can make an important contribution to the emerging three-dimensional picture of children's mathematical thinking. In this way staff can plan to play an active role in taking children's mathematical learning forward. The dynamic nature of education is such that in the process staff will themselves learn more, both about mathematics and about learning.

Planning for mathematical learning and thinking

Planning in the early years has been subject to a range of pressures to become more objectives driven. This has been true of all areas of learning but the pressure for increased formality in planning for mathematical development has been equalled only by planning for literacy. While it is right that practitioners should be accountable to government and to parents it is also vital to maintain a sense of what is right for children. Planning for successful mathematical learning must take account of what we know of successful learning in general – that it is playful, dynamic, social and constantly seeking enjoyment and challenge. Planning must therefore be responsive to children's interests and understanding. It must allow the time and space for play, flexibility and interaction.

Political pressures

> In accepting a developmental approach to the curriculum for young children, the highest priority must be given to the needs and development of the individual child.
>
> (Lally 1991: 86)

For those who view the development of young children and the provision of a curriculum designed to support that development appropriately as paramount, the current political climate creates conflicts which some find difficult to resolve. In practice there are many downward pressures on those who work with young children to work towards the objectives set and defined for older children. Indeed, it has been said that pressure emanating from universities is shaping the curriculum of the nursery. A story told by Pat Gura and Tina Bruce of an observation from the Froebel Blockplay Research Project serves as a reminder of the ineptness of this stance:

> A recent three-year-old arrival to the nursery class had been watching with awe-struck admiration as an older child was

completing a tall and magnificent block structure by standing on a stepladder. The newcomer was anxious to emulate this daring achievement, picked up a block, climbed to the top of the ladder and asked, 'Can I start here?'

The introduction of the foundation stage (QCA 2000) has provided early years' practitioners with the opportunity to influence primary practice. For example, as Edgington (2004) points out the introduction of the Foundation Stage Profile (QCA/DfES 2003) 'highlighted the gulf between nursery and reception class assessment practice' since the latter had relatively little experience of 'observation-based evidence'.

In some early childhood settings, adults now feel that their planning must be all about specific objectives. To do this, to define specific learning objectives divorced from the learning needs of children, is to fly in the face of two centuries of growth in the understanding of young children's minds. As early childhood practitioners, we face a difficult task. We need to place, side by side, the learning needs of children and the things that society expects them to know. We should never lose sight of the fact that children must become not only literate and numerate but flexible, resourceful and confident mathematicians.

Subject knowledge

Aubrey (1994: 68) comments that in the area of mathematics, teachers are helped to plan in such a way as to enable them to react to children's learning needs if they are confident in the relevant subject knowledge. She says they will then have a mental plan or agenda of what they hope children will learn and a curriculum script so that they know how to turn their subject knowledge into effective classroom practice. The problem with mathematics is that many of the adults who work with young children lack confidence in their own abilities in this area of the curriculum. This lack of confidence can lead practitioners to over-formalize and fail to pick up on informal opportunities to develop mathematical understanding.

Subject knowledge can help those who work with young children to be more relaxed about helping them to achieve it. Gura (1994) has criticized a subject-based approach. While recognizing the value of subject expertise, her concerns are about the way in which the curriculum for young children becomes shaped by the subjects, rather than building on what we know of young children's learning. Aubrey (1994) says that subject specialists in the early years tend to teach their specialist area more dynamically, represent the subject in more varied ways, encourage and respond more fully to children's questions and comments. Her views are in part echoed by Menmuir and Adams (1997: 34):

These intentions cannot be too specific or they may limit the inquiry but the better the underlying understanding of maths which the adult possesses, the easier it is to recognise the mathematical potential of a wide range of children's persistent concerns.

It is vital that early childhood specialism is equally valued alongside subject expertise, as Menmuir and Adams intimate. Exploring the role of subject knowledge in Reggio Emilia, where each school employs an *atelierista* or art specialist, Pound and Gura (1997: 27) write:

It is clear that when expertise is co-ordinated, the effects, as in Reggio Emilia, are felt not only in terms of particular areas of knowledge and skill but in the connections which can be made between ideas and people.

Approaches to planning

At all stages of planning it is vital that teachers create activities that are engaging and interesting in their own right and that offer a real-life context for each aspect of maths.

(Lewis 1996: 179)

Planning for mathematics needs to happen at many levels. Over the course of a year or more, depending on how long most children attend the setting, there will be a range of areas that you will wish children to experience. These will include both the content curriculum – pattern and the search for relationships, measurement (including time), shape and space, counting (including work on money) – and the learning curriculum. Little of this planned mathematical activity will happen in isolation. The ongoing themes of children's education as a whole will be exploited and developed to ensure that each child's entitlement to the way of knowing and understanding the world which is mathematics is guaranteed.

Over the course of a month or a half term, some specific plans will be laid to address these broad areas. For example, plans to visit a local farm will lead to planning for specific opportunities for mathematical development, among other things. Individual children will connect with these opportunities in different ways. To aid clearing up and to give a context for using numbers, 4-year-old James's teacher prepared small boxes which fitted inside the normal large storage trays. Attractively presented, each small box was labelled with a photograph and caption showing how many and what type of animal should be placed in it. James enjoyed playing with the small-world materials but was horrified when it was suggested to him that he might use these to make sure that all the farm animals were safely tidied away. 'I don't know numbers,' he said. Wisely the teacher did not press his immediate involvement but began to observe. Over time the staff team realized that he had quite a lot of number knowledge but that he lacked confidence in using it because he was not as knowledgeable as his older sister. Future planning addressed his particular needs alongside the options for developing mathematics around the current theme or topic.

At this stage of education, structure is something which must exist in the *mind* of the adult – it must not be allowed to become an obstacle to learning. Having planned the content and learning curricula, the learning needs of the children must remain of paramount importance. Skilled teachers will ensure that the curriculum for each child matches their developmental needs by selecting material from the pre-planned components. When the planned learning opportunities are based on sensitive observation of children they will generally be developmentally appropriate. Sometimes unplanned chances to teach aspects of the planned content or learning curriculum will emerge. On other occasions, teachers will need to abandon planned activities, seeking other teaching requirements when children will be more receptive. There can be no justification for imposing on little children a series of undifferentiated worksheets. Nor should we believe that simply moving children in groups around a series of narrow mathematical tasks which are not designed to meet the specific learning needs of any of them will support their mathematical development. Learning must build on what they know and must therefore be individualized. 'Individualized' does not mean isolated and it certainly does not rule out the importance of joint discussions about mathematics – any more than the fact that children are at different stages of understanding stories means that they all have to have individual stories. Rather adults will need to be aware that different children will benefit differently from group sessions.

Gifford (1995) is critical of an approach to planning for mathematics which is unclear about objectives. She suggests that those who claim that 'mathematics is everywhere' often fail to intervene appropriately and that 'nursery practitioners' negative attitudes [prevent] them seeing mathematics as pleasurable or informal'. They may then fail to identify and exploit opportunities to support mathematical thinking and development. These claims would seem to be justified but in the light of evidence that nursery schools and integrated centres appear to offer a more effective mathematical experience than provision in nursery classes or private and voluntary settings (Sammons *et al*. 2002), and that nursery schools and integrated centres seem most likely to offer a more child-centred provision, as evidenced by the use of worksheets (Worthington and Carruthers 2003), these claims perhaps need to be reconsidered. While it is clearly important to have objectives, it is also vital to address the learning needs of young children which demand that practitioners teach them at times when they can do so playfully, when it is relevant to the child and in ways that enable them to connect mathematical with other learning. If practitioners lack the confidence or knowledge to do this effectively then it is that gap which must be addressed.

Supporting mathematical learning and thinking

Adults will have to wear a good many hats in undertaking their role of supporting mathematical learning and thinking. It is a broad issue and one which cannot be divorced from all the other support which they must give as children grow and develop as learners in all areas of experience and understanding. Many of the aspects discussed below are common to all other areas of learning. All the aspects in the sections that follow require planning – even apparently spontaneous intervention requires that staff have planned to ensure that children can be as independent as possible and that staff have time to make decisions about intervention.

Creating an ethos for mathematical learning

This demands the creation of an atmosphere within the classroom which values creative, flexible thought and which promotes approaches which will give lifelong support to thinking mathematically. It will, as a by-product, support other kinds of learning. Lewis (1996: 179) suggests that it is the role of the early childhood educator to develop a climate for learning. In such an ethos, children are enabled to take responsibilities and intellectual risks, to be independent and to make choices. Such a setting will be mutually supportive and will promote trust among its members. This will involve the professional in building on the children's own ideas. From them discussion, exploration, thought and imagination will all flow. Menmuir and Adams (1997) identify key elements in making enquiry happen. These include listening to and observing children and encouraging them to share their successes. Such encouragement will come through talking to parents and carers about what they have achieved. It will come through records, accessible to parents and children, which celebrate mathematical achievement in its broadest sense. It may come through displays in the classroom or early years setting giving a high profile to things that children have said about numbers or made using mathematical ideas. Books made by adults and children together about investigations or problem-solving activities will provide another strategy for sharing children's mathematical successes.

An important part of creating an ethos for mathematical learning is in ensuring that children have adults to whom they readily refer. Munn and Schaffer (1993) studied young children in day nurseries. They emphasize the value of a key worker system, with children assigned to one specific adult. They also suggest that teachers should stress early numeracy experiences, as they do with literacy. Teachers' ability to do so depended on their understanding of the role of talk and interaction in promoting children's mathematical learning.

Managing resources for mathematical learning

Since as we have seen mathematical learning is embedded in everyday experiences and since mathematical development is closely linked to development in all other areas of the curriculum many of the resources needed to support mathematical understanding will be found in all areas of provision. However, it is useful to have a focal point where children can find the resources they need gathered in one place. Hill (in Marsden and Woodbridge 2005: 17–18) describes the development of what the children came to call the 'maths shelves' in the reception classes where staff were seeking to create a more meaningful curriculum. She writes:

> We wanted to make a difference to the children's thinking and learning. We wanted to give them opportunities to make connections, to talk about their learning and, most of all, to be 'playful' . . . The maths area was one of the last to be developed. Why was this area last? Did we think the children would only achieve by having a diet of teacher-directed, and sometimes unconnected, activities? . . . Weeks of discussion, planning and organizing saw the maths table (where we used to put out equipment that we had chosen) disappear and the maths area evolve. We moved a small shelving unit into the area, purchased a few essential items and we had moved off the 'start' line . . .
>
> We wanted to link some of the maths equipment to our topic . . . it

was winter so we used penguins, polar bears, snow . . . We had 30 silver stars and 30 snowflakes . . . We had a variety of dice and spinners, sets of numbers to 10, 20 and 30, numberlines, some 2D and 3D shapes, whiteboards, writing equipment, number books and *One Snowy Night* by Nick Butterworth, a number story with toys. The shelves were full as was the floor area around them. The children were already used to choosing from various baskets and boxes in the other areas of provision areas and although this area was always busy, it was also always tidy.

What initially amazed the adults was the length of time children spent at the maths shelves and the level of competence at which they worked. Both were greater than previously observed. The children were 'playing' at maths – we had set the area up together, they knew the focus was maths and that was what they were doing.

Gifford (1995) suggests the inclusion of structured resources, including Pattern Blocks and Poleidoblocs, a variety of numerals, collections of recourse such as buttons, shells, stones and jewels – a firm favourite. Like Hill, she favours the inclusion of materials for children to make up their own games. Skinner (2005) highlights the importance of making ICT resources available. Although she is writing about 'Maths Outdoors' she suggests that mobile phones and walkie talkies, digital cameras and calculators can all contribute to mathematical learning. This would argue for making such resources available indoors and out.

In addition to a dedicated mathematics area, mathematical development will be supported by enriching the whole environment. Worthington and Carruthers (2003: 142) with their emphasis on writing and drawing suggest that including some of the following to the graphics area will promote mathematical recording:

- rulers
- calculator
- calendar
- measuring tape
- numberlines (different lengths)
- stamps
- shapes
- tickets
- cheque book
- cut out numbers
- clock
- birthday cards
- petty cash receipts

- raffle tickets
- recipes.

In similar vein, Tucker (2005) recommends adding mathematical resources to role-play areas and other imaginative play situations. This might mean including resources for a birthday party in the home corner, different sized bedding, clothes and buttons for doll play and dressing-up.

In short, managing resources for mathematical development requires:

- dedicated provision in the maths area and in access to such resources for outdoor play
- generalized provision in all other areas of provision, with practitioners checking that the mathematical aspect of what is offered to children is made more visible
- themed provision e.g. highlighting pattern in all areas of provision.

Holding high but attainable expectations

Mathematical learning will be supported by having high expectations – like all developmental processes mathematical thinking develops, to a large extent, in response to the cultural context of the child. If we work to create a classroom where the implicit expectation is that children are destined to be competent and confident mathematicians in the broadest sense, then we are well on the way to helping them achieve that. Part of having high expectations lies in not giving too much praise. The repetitive use of phrases such as 'That's lovely, dear!' and 'That's super!' can be patronizing and may not enable children to build on their successes or avoid failure in the future. Praise of this sort does not provide children with any information that will allow them to develop the strengths of what they have achieved. It can also make children feel that we are too easily pleased and not provide any incentive to struggle with ideas. Constructive criticism is, however, important and is most effective when it focuses on positive aspects. Where adults comment on the things which children have done well – used a new strategy, managed to remember something previously discussed, successfully matched things up, identified a pattern – this allows children to reflect on what they have done and do it again. At some points, children will benefit from an addition to these positive comments which asks them to reflect further – perhaps adding 'Can you think of any other ways of doing that?' or 'Is that the only pattern you can see?' The combination of specific praise and challenge can encourage children to ask more of themselves.

With young children, who are so vulnerable to the intentions of adults and so anxious to please, it is easy to promote 'prediction and other mathematical thinking processes by drawing attention to them as they arise' (Lewis 1996: 179). We must take care that we do not signal to children the overriding importance of things which may inhibit their long-term development as mathematicians. They are all too eager to please us and if we signal that doing pages of sums is what we most value, many will want to do that. Girls, in particular, may enjoy keeping busy, doing unchallenging but safe activities, which frequently result in praise and rows of ticks. High expectations are not all about getting things right. If children do not make mistakes, they will not be learning. Their errors show adults what their thinking is and thus enables them to support children's learning.

Sustained shared thinking

Clarke and Atkinson (1996) emphasize the importance of talk in promoting mathematical thinking. Adults, they suggest, should monitor their own contributions and use tangible materials to support verbal explanations, particularly for young children, those learning English as an additional language and those who may be experiencing language delay or disorders. They suggest encouraging children to talk about their current understanding and to explore things they do not understand.

The tension between providing visual cues and encouraging children to rely on thought without external aids should be explored. The work of Martin Hughes (1986a) provides a good model. Habit and routine played a part in the process he established. Teachers might begin by putting, for example, three blocks into a bag, making their actions highly visible. They might add three more – with larger-than-life actions so that all children will be aware exactly what has happened. This game, for this is what it should be, may be played over a considerable period. Only when children are really familiar with it should the prop of the actual blocks be pulled away, so that those who are unsure can still gain enjoyment. If the group is small enough to ensure that no one has to wait too long for a turn, harder challenges may be offered to individual children. A balance needs to be struck between keeping the group, on the one hand, large and diverse enough so that children are exposed to a range of understandings and, on the other hand, compact enough for children to feel personally involved.

Hill (in Marsden and Woodbridge 2005: 79) suggests that levels and quality of children's sustained shared thinking rise dramatically when:

- they are offered well-organised and stimulating resources that reflect the children's natural interests
- they are given time to be playful, in a secure environment, which allows them to take risks and make connections in their learning
- they are assisted by reflective and questioning adults and, of course, by all the other thinking children in the class.

Open-ended questions are more effective than closed ones but as Gifford (2005b) observes: 'More indirect and less confrontational strategies are required for younger children . . . [and] statements provoked more discussion than questioning.' Commenting on the size of the building that children have constructed with the blocks is more likely to develop into sustained conversation/thinking than a closed question such as 'How many cylinders have you used?' Gifford (2005b) also recommends the use of humour in conversations with children and the use of puppets – since puppets can ask questions and make mistakes that would not ring true if made directly by the adult.

Intervening or interfering?

Clarke and Atkinson (1996) suggest that children should be encouraged to offer explanations to each other, accepting everyone's contribution, thus keeping adult intervention in such conversations to a minimum. Lewis (1996: 179) also urges against intervention when it is concerned with stepping in when children are heading for mistakes. Sometimes voicing their thinking can of itself help children to identify the inconsistencies in their own understanding.

Intervention is, however, vital in many contexts. Adults can provide explanations, sometimes supported by analogies to help make the explanations clearer. Aubrey (1994: 68) claims that adults' subject knowledge plays a crucial role in their ability to do this effectively. They will have a key role in helping children to make connections, which will include the links with existing knowledge as well as the links with other areas of experience. When talking about bygone events, discussing with children the ways in which time is quantified, adults can encourage children to wrestle with that very complex concept. Although young children have very hazy ideas of distance – how many of us have experienced, either as a child or as a parent, the woebegone cry of 'Are we there yet?' – discussion about how far it is to the post office or Spain or India gives the adult an insight into the child's understanding. It also gives children an opportunity to test out their views on a sympathetic audience and to compare and modify their view in the light of what other children think.

Questioning is a common intervention strategy. It works best in promoting mathematical thought if the questions are open. A closed question which really only has one right answer – 'How many sheep are there?' – may tell us whether children can count to a specific number, unless they are enjoying being able to tell a sheep from a lamb. However, if they resent the question as being too obvious, or for some other more hidden reason, it will tell us little. Wood (1991) reminds us that questioning is not a wholly productive method of teaching young children. He suggests that children as young as 4 are often aware when adults already know the answer to the questions they ask. He continues:

> The less a teacher interrogates children, the more likely they are to listen to, make contributions about and ask questions of what the other children say . . . The extent to which a child reveals his or her own ideas and seeks information is thus inversely proportional to the frequency of teacher questions – and this finding embraces studies of pre-school children through to 16-year-olds, deaf children and children acquiring English as a second language.
>
> (Wood 1991: 115)

Open questions which children recognize as having a variety of answers and to which we genuinely do not have a specific answer will motivate thought and stimulate a spirit of enquiry. Lewis (1996: 179) suggests questioning *right* answers so that children develop the habit of justifying and explaining their views.

Intervening for equality of opportunity

Teachers and other professionals will need to evaluate their practice in the light of the need to ensure equality of opportunity. As Kelly (1994: 22) writes, citing Warnock:

> There is a difference between claiming that everyone has an equal right to education and that everyone has a right to equal education. In a democratic society 'entitlement' should mean more than entitlement to access; it should mean entitlement to full and appropriate provision.

The disabled, those with marked mathematical aptitude, girls and boys, those for whom English is an additional language and those of all social classes and levels of privilege have a right to an education that makes them not simply numerate but able to think mathematically. They also should be given access to the exciting and challenging aspects of mathematics which will remain for ever closed to most of today's adult population. Children who cannot move freely may enjoy the power of commanding a computer-controlled robot or vehicle. Those who are in the early stages of learning English will benefit from a chance to talk in their first language with their peers about the ideas and concepts they are being encouraged to develop in English.

Adults' evaluation will include a check to ensure that the needs of all the learners in the class are being met. Traditionally mathematics has been seen as an area in which boys excel and free choice is sometimes criticized as merely prolonging stereotypical behaviour. Parkin's (1991: 63) observations in her classroom led her to the following conclusions:

> The free choice of young infants does not differ significantly between girls and boys but there is a difference in the way boys and girls behave and in the way they use resources. Girls' behaviour prevents them participating equally with boys in many problem-solving and other practical classroom activities but their behaviour is advantageous to other expressions of mathematical concepts. In certain mathematical activities girls perform as well as and sometimes better than boys.

In the blockplay project (Gura 1992) adults found that where they involved themselves in children's play and where children were given time and space to explore the materials exhaustively stereotypical behaviour disappeared.

If children are not making progress is it because the curriculum has not engaged them? Cousins (1990: 30–31) describes Sonnyboy's difficulties in accessing the curriculum of his reception class:

> He was scathing about the absence of real money in the classroom shop; couldn't fathom out what was meant by playtime; questioned why school scissors were always blunt and didn't see why you couldn't eat snacks when you felt hungry. He put on extra clothes for PE because it was cold in the hall and decided assembly was the time to dream . . . School time caused him a lot of trouble . . .

Writers in Britain and abroad have documented social class differences in young children's mathematical achievement around the age of compulsory schooling (Hughes 1986a; Young-Loveridge 1987), with children from advantaged socio-economic circumstances demonstrating greater levels of knowledge. Results nationally throughout the years of schooling reflect this difference. However, the research of Tizard et al. (1988)

suggested that even when children from disadvantaged groups entered school with higher measured levels of achievement they did ultimately less well than other more advantaged children. Walkerdine (1989) offers explanations which have to do with the constraints which poverty and low status impose on families. Others would suggest that teachers have lower expectations of children in disadvantaged circumstances. There are no easy answers to these complex findings, but if equality of access has any meaning at all, practitioners have a responsibility to ensure that every aspect of the child's previous experience is valued and developed.

Scaffolding

Bruner (1983: 60) picks up Vygotsky's notion of *scaffolding* and empha-sizes the importance of adults playing a fully participatory role in children's learning. He writes:

> If the teacher . . . were to have a motto, it would surely be where before there was a spectator, let there now be a participant. One . . . provides a scaffold to ensure that the child's ineptitudes can be rescued by appropriate intervention, and then removes the scaffold part by part as the reciprocal structure can stand on its own.

Wood (1991: 109) describes this as *leading by following,* meaning that scaffolds work best when they surround a structure that the child is interested in scaling. Scaffolding is a vital element in creating a devel-opmentally appropriate curriculum. Wood (1991: 111) further reminds us that children as young as 9 months understand that adults (or older children) can be enlisted to offer the scaffold or support that they need to achieve something they want to do. At this tender age they are already capable of demonstrating that fierce combination of independence and interdependence that will mark out the effective learner.

Hutchin (1996: 104) offers helpful insights into some of the effective ways in which adults can scaffold children's experiences. She describes Faisal's mathematical development at the age of 3 years 3 months, and outlines what she sees as the implications for teaching:

Observation on Faisal:	Implications for teaching
F. lined up cars parallel to each other in rows, sorted out all the small cuboid blocks and lined them up similarly, talking in Bengali as he did this.	Build on interest in parallel lines and lengths in lots of situations - e.g. rolling dough, collage, train set, large blocks outside.
Made a wall two rows with milk cartons at milk table, later made a similar pattern with blocks. Fitted cars on a flat board in rows covering all of surface, counted to 3 in English.	Draw his models to show him the patterns he makes.
When drawing, drew parallel horizontal lines on paper, usually doing several at one time.	Continue interest in block play.

What is particularly interesting about the implications for teaching is the suggestion that the teacher should draw Faisal's model. Hutchin does not suggest that Faisal should be asked to do this, since Faisal has already represented his ideas The teacher's drawings are to be used to focus his attention on a particular teaching point – not as a mechanism for keeping him at the model table for longer. It is the opportunity for interactive dialogue which is seen as important.

Demonstrating mathematical behaviour

Of great importance is the role that adults play as mathematicians themselves in supporting young children's mathematical learning. This will involve lifelong learning both about mathematics and about the process of learning itself. It will also involve modelling mathematical behaviour. Demonstrating the strategies used when counting up the dinner numbers or totalling the photograph money, writing number operations as you do them and so on will help children to see where and how we use mathematics.

Merttens (1996: 21–2) comments on the role that Piaget's work has played in undervaluing the role of adults in promoting mathematical thinking and in over-emphasizing the importance of commercially pro-duced materials:

Piaget's emphasis on children as lone individuals, all necessarily working at their own pace . . . hindered the role that interaction with peers played in the learning process . . . and obstructed the development of children's ability to make decisions about what they do, how and when – in short to think mathematically.

Merttens (1996: 10) also emphasizes that 'teaching is not telling'. She describes it as an *interactive process*, a dialogue. Unfortunately, from the point of view of those who care for and educate very young children, these useful statements are preceded by a section where the teacher's role in instructing, modelling, explaining, questioning and narrating is explored, in that order. It is a pity that she begins with instruction since for young children that is rarely a good starting point. Their questions and the adults' answers, explanations and illustrative stories are far more effective. Instruction, as discussed earlier, is most effective when it begins with the child's concerns. The younger the child, the more important it is that adults' instruction matches the child's immediate needs.

Observing, planning and supporting

A nursery unit had been focusing on boats and were placing a special emphasis on *Mr Gumpy's Outing* (Burningham 1972) with props to support role play, materials for small-world play and magnetic cut-outs to use on a story board. Some children had been making boats, and during a group story session the nursery nurse discussed with them the boats that some of the children had made. Several of the children had difficulty in remembering the word for the sail. Suddenly 3-year-old Danny remembered it: 'It's a triangle sail!' Each time the nursery nurse commented on a sail, he would add that it was a triangle. At the team meeting the nursery nurse talked to the rest of the team about the session. It was decided that some plastic boats, some of which had square sails, would be put in the water tray and that Danny would be invited to join in the making of a book about boats using pictures of boats with a range of sails in order to help him clarify the meaning of the two words.

Ten-month-old Siân was observed to enjoy playing with things that rolled. Her key worker talked to Siân's parent about it, who said that she had a small clear plastic ball at home with bells inside. She liked to push it with her hand and crawl after it. Staff asked the parent if he would like to bring it in to the nursery. They found a similar one with coloured fish inside. Siân's enjoyment of the similarities and differences was evident.

Four-year-old Mei enjoyed using a computer program which required children to match a number of objects to a number symbol. If the number of objects displayed did not match, some more could be added by pressing the space bar, or taken away by pressing the delete key. Mei's strategy was to empty the box on the screen by pressing the delete key and then to put in as many as she needed. So, for example, if the number was 8 but six objects were displayed she would delete all six and then count to 8 as she added in objects. Staff had observed this over a period of several days but then noticed that in checking how many cartons of milk were left she was able to count on. She had been asked to check how many cartons were left on the trolley, which she did, telling staff that there were six. She then added, however, that there were two more on the table so there were eight altogether. In order to help her to connect her understanding to the computer program, the teacher prepared an activity for a small group following a story session. Specific numbers of objects were hidden in a bag and a small number added. Among the objects used were included some of the things that were used on the computer program in order to help Mei to transfer her understanding.

Summary

Those who recognize the need to offer young children a developmentally appropriate curriculum seek to build on the 'natural' ways of learning which operate between young children and their parents or carers (Papousek and Papousek 1987). Where parents are under stress, this unconsciously driven pattern of interaction, where parents build on what they see children do and offer support for them to do things which are just a little beyond their capability, may break down.

Professional carers and educators work to conflicting sets of demands and may be less focused in their intentions than parents. They have also to care for larger numbers of children with less intimate knowledge than parents have. Planning therefore becomes of vital importance since it allows parents to negotiate where potential conflicts arise and the practitioners themselves to ensure that entitlements are offered to all.

6

Parents and professionals working together

Children need 'warm demanders' if they are to thrive (Ball 1994: 43).

'Partnerships' has become an easy word: on all sides we are exhorted to develop them – business partnerships, development partnerships and, not least, home–school partnerships. Fortunately, overuse of the word does not make them less valuable, but neither does it make them any easier to achieve. Whether easy or difficult to achieve, partnership between the parents of young children and those who work with them in early years settings is not negotiable – it is absolutely essential. The knowledge which parents have of their own children's experiences, preferences and growing understanding is vital to staff's awareness. The records which staff keep of children's growing understanding provides an important bridge, giving parents insight into the work of the early years setting. In relation to mathematics it becomes even more important, since so often the experiences of parents lead them to look for formal recording or sums as evidence of mathematics. Observations and assessments then support the close contact between the two groups responsible for the child's care and education which is essential if the child is to make the necessary connections between experiences at home and those elsewhere. Hughes (1986b: 36) writes:

> Children grow up within a closely linked network of people, based on their family, which makes up their community. Much of children's early learning takes place within this network. When they start school, children find themselves in a very different world,

from which there are few links either to their own community or to the kind of knowledge they have acquired within that community. One of the tasks of school must be to help children create these links. This will not be an easy task, and schools will need all the help they can get – particularly from parents.

What both family and workers have in common is that they want the best for the child. Among workers, teachers and others concerned with children's care and education within an institution, this concern is professional and largely objective. Among parents and others close to children within the close-knit circle of family and friends this desire is subjective and passionate. This is its strength (Bronfenbrenner 1979).

The educational benefits of contact between home and other carers and educators have been well expressed in a number of studies. Widlake and Macleod (1984: 49) quote the words of an unnamed community educator in the United States:

> There is a whole book of studies . . . that makes very interesting reading. Fifty-five pages of short versions of studies that say when parents take any interest in schooling, the kids' ranks go up; even if they only spend ten minutes a day talking about school; even if they only wish the kids a good day and remind them to 'work hard today'.

One of the less well-known factors in the very well-publicized long-term effects of the High/Scope Project was the close involvement of parents. Staff were given significant allocations of time to make home visits, to develop contact and to discuss children's progress with their parents.

Barriers to partnership

There are many things that make partnership difficult. One is the lack of training among professionals for working *with* parents. There is a danger that in a profession with low status (and sometimes low morale), some will seek to hold on to the small amount of power that they have and will not wish to share it with parents. Pugh and De'ath (1984) has commented on the fact that professionals often unwittingly damage parents' self-confidence. If this is true in general, it is certainly true about mathematics. Parents as a representative part of the population will not be exempt from the insecurity that many people feel about their ability to make use of mathematics in their everyday lives. On top of that insecurity, Burton (1994: 124) reminds us that 'parents have to make two major shifts in their thinking'.

First, *what* children learn, what is called mathematics, is likely to look very different for all but the youngest parents from what they themselves experienced at school. Second, *how* children are taught, and the organization of the classroom including mathematical resources, is likely to differ from some parents' very unhappy memories of mathematics teaching. Paradoxically, even with widespread evidence that approaches to mathematics which have been neither successful nor enjoyable many parents favour teaching like that which they themselves experienced.

A further barrier to partnership in relation to the development of children's mathematical thinking is alluded to by Browne (1991: 18). She focuses on the difficulties for early childhood practitioners in teaching science, but in doing so highlights the common issues raised in relation to mathematics. Practitioners are said to be afraid of not being able to answer children's questions or of not being able to help children find their own answers. They are, moreover, frightened of the mathematics that might be involved in young children's science questions. The combination of parental distrust of change in the teaching of mathematics and practitioners' lack of confidence will magnify the difficulties associated with partnership and make it unlikely that professionals will feel able either to negotiate change or to convince parents of a need to do so.

Parents' views of course should not be seen as a homogeneous whole. Their views will form a continuum from those who fear mathematics and who do not mind if their children are not good at it to those who have very high expectations. Clemson and Clemson (1994: 23) suggest that young children have an implicit sense of their parents' views of mathematics. Some will know that their parents do not like mathematics. Some will have gained the impression that mathematics is hard while others will be equally sure that it is easy, especially boys. For some, to be good at counting and sums will be seen as important; while for others, they will be an irrelevance. Some will be very clear that this is an area in which their parents wish them to succeed, even though it is hard. The views of parents interviewed by Atkinson (1992: 165) reflect a similar range:

> I panic about maths. As I am talking to you now my heart is pounding . . . if maths is mentioned, I go all hot and cold. I cannot help my own children, because I panic as soon as they tell me the problem. I want them to understand not just be told to learn it by rote . . . Most of all I don't want them to panic like I did.
>
> I wasn't any good at maths so I don't suppose my child will be either.

They do things like cooking at school, and lots of practical maths, but now she is seven, I want her to get on with some real maths.

I don't want my child to suffer what I went through. I want her to enjoy it and understand it.

I don't approve of all this messing about with shapes and cubes.

Supporting partnership

Because we know that children from families who give mathematics a high profile in their day-to-day lives (Young-Loveridge 1989) develop a greater enthusiasm for mathematics, early childhood practitioners should be doing all they can to encourage parents to play games, talk about time, and draw children's attention to calendars, money and telephone numbers when they are using them. Early childhood educators have, however, an additional responsibility, namely to replicate these conditions which lead to children becoming *young experts* (Young-Loveridge 1989). Where young children are in full-day care it is especially important that they are given frequent and varied opportunities to use the real-life mathematics prevalent in the real-life situation of the home: in cooking, handling money, checking bus numbers for journeys, remembering phone numbers and making sure that there are sufficient quantities of everything.

Home and parents offer excellent opportunities for real-life contexts for mathematics, although as Gifford (1995) points out, the opportunities for experiencing, for example, the mathematics of cooking, laying the table or even shopping are not available in all homes. While we may agree that 'it is the school's role to introduce children to a way of thinking and knowing the world which is independent of their own experiences' (Tizard and Hughes 1984: 263), this can only be achieved if schools value and build on the real experiences that children have. Independence from their own experiences can only come about when we have encouraged children to see the connections between their contextualized learning and the more abstract understandings we wish them to move towards. The attitude of their parents is part of that link.

A further example of where we may fail to build on children's prior learning may lie in the emphasis given to sorting, matching and ordering, claims Womack (1993). He writes that 'it is more than likely that the average home environment provides a sufficient variety of these activities'. Others (Gifford 1995; Macnamara 1996; Merttens 1996) support him in thinking that the early emphasis given to these activities, particularly in reception classes, represents a failure to recognize children's prior experiences.

The insecurities that exist on both parts can lead to unrealistic demands – some low expectations from professionals, as Womack's work seems to indicate, and some unhelpful expectations on the part of parents. One parent, quoted in Atkinson (1992: 165) as saying, 'You're failing my child. She is four, in the nursery, and she doesn't know her tables yet,' provides an example.

Somehow the oft-quoted words of the Cockcroft Report (DES 1982; cited in Lewis 1996: 173) have not gained much credence:

Albeit with the best of intentions, parents can exert undesirable pressure on teachers to introduce written recording in mathematics . . . A premature start on formal, written arithmetic is likely to delay progress rather than hasten it.

There can be no doubt that the political emphasis on high achievement has increased parental anxiety. In a study by David (1992) the views of Belgian and British parents on pre-school education were compared. The former placed an emphasis on children developing naturally, while British parents placed importance on the early development of reading and writing. Cox and Sanders (1994: 176) suggest that this shows a need for nursery educators to demonstrate to parents that the informal learning experiences that characterize early childhood education yield real and observable benefits for the children, even though they precede the more formal achievements.

The Rumbold Report (DES 1990: para. 100) underlines this point:

What is needed is for educators to be able and willing to explain to parents how the experiences offered to children contribute to their learning, and to describe how their children are progressing . . . They must ensure that they have the necessary skills to work effectively with parents . . . There is much to be done if early childhood education is to make its contribution to improving the quality of mathematical education both in what actually happens in early childhood settings but also in convincing parents of the reasons for doing what we do in early childhood settings. This will not be easy since many practitioners find it very difficult to articulate the rationale for the way in which they work.

Developing communication with parents

For many parents, working alongside children in an early years setting can help them to understand what teaching staff are trying to achieve. They may supervise specific activities, help to display work, work with children on the computer or read to them. This can be particularly useful where the parent has worries about too much play and not enough work, although, as the parent quoted by Atkinson (1992: 165) shows, this strategy is by no means foolproof. The parent says, 'I go in to help some days and they ask me to play maths games. I quite enjoy doing that and the children love it, but it is not real maths, is it?' Parents need to have explained the purpose of what they are being asked to do. One wonders whether this parent had been asked, for example, to observe the strategies that children were using or to encourage children to guess the number of spots on the dice before counting them in order to promote speed, estimation and confidence.

With older children, Burton (1994) recommends encouraging them to record their work (in, for example, scoring games or describing how sweets have been fairly distributed) in order to show their parents what they have been doing. She also suggests that teachers make sure that children are aware of the mathematics they have been doing so that they are able to tell their parents about it. In the case of younger children, adults working with them will need to undertake this kind of link themselves. This is partly because children may not have the language to do it successfully, but it is also because such conversations give parents an opportunity to raise questions and to share views with staff.

From these conversations, staff may decide that it would be helpful to focus on certain aspects of the mathematics curriculum. In order to do this they may develop parent workshops or open evenings where parents may be given the chance to use equipment and generally try out some of the experiences their children are having. In some nurseries, leaflets raising pertinent issues are published and distributed to parents.

Regular information about the mathematics curriculum may be conveyed to parents. Many early years settings have a curriculum noticeboard or regular newsletter to keep parents up to date with plans for all areas of the curriculum including mathematics. Booklets outlining the approach to maths taken by staff can also be helpful.

For example, many early years settings produce booklets for parents to help them support their own children's mathematical development. These may include examples of what the school does to promote mathematical thinking, and offer ideas for ways in which parents can help at home. Similarly, the HBJ Mathematics scheme (Kerslake *et al.* 1990) includes draft format letters to parents explaining what aspect of mathematics is to be taught during the coming half term. The letter for each topic includes four headings: 'What we will be doing'; 'Why we will be doing it'; 'How you can help'; and 'Try this at home!'. Early Education (Skinner and Ebbutt nd) produces and distributes free of charge a short pamphlet entitled 'Maths is Everywhere' designed specifically for parents which includes excellent advice on supporting young children's mathematical development.

Instead of simply informing parents about the mathematics curriculum, early childhood educators could try asking for their suggestions. Again the ensuing conversations may do much to promote mutual understanding, as can the practice of inviting parents to contribute to their child's own record. Parents' insights into children's mathematical understanding may take a different stance than those contributed by professionals and the merging of ideas can be helpful. This two-way exchange of ideas can be especially helpful where the culture of the home and that of the school differ. Understandings of mathematics are likely to be different among families and workers, but this gulf may be particularly significant where parents have been educated outside Britain. We should not assume that the differences are based on socio-economic differences. What appears to be significant is the general interest and involvement of parents and carers (Sammons *et al.* 2002). Staff will need to show particular sensitivity and be willing to spend time explaining why mathematics is being approached in the way that it is. For their part, parents will need to give staff insight into what is being done at home.

Home reading schemes, with children regularly borrowing books, are well established in many early years settings. An increasingly important way of developing shared understandings with parents about children's mathematical thinking and knowledge is to encourage children to take activities such as investigations, games and puzzles home to share with their family. Burton (1994: 131) quotes from a letter to parents designed to encourage their involvement in what is sometimes called an IMPACT scheme:

> The home is where a child's maths education begins. It also provides a wealth of opportunities for maths activities and games. Here, you and your child can be together in a relaxed setting which is relevant to the child. It also offers you a chance to share maths with your child without too much extra effort!

The involvement of parents can be further enhanced if parents themselves are active in making games and resources for a home lending scheme. Simple board games with a variety of dice – some with spots, some with numbers, some with pictures and some even with words – are simple to play at home and can be undertaken by older brothers and sisters as well as parents and grandparents. The literacy packs (a book together with props, which might be a toy related to the story, a relevant game or a set of small characters which represent the characters in the book) – sometimes called story sacks – produced by some nurseries and schools to support reading at home can have applications for developing mathematical understanding. The set of animals which accompanies *Rosie's Walk* (Hutchins 1968) in such a pack, for example, offers lots of opportunities for mathematical discussion and language. Similarly, some early years settings produce props for number rhymes including such favourites as 'Five fat sausages sizzling in a pan' (sausages made from tights fastened with Velcro to a cardboard frying pan) and 'Five little speckled frogs'. These props are generally confined to the early years classroom but some parents might be happy to make replicas which could be used at home – thus sharing familiar songs and rhymes as well as mathematics. Hand-manufactured books with a mathematical theme, perhaps illustrating a recent educational visit focusing on shape, depicting activities where patterns are discernible or encouraging counting of resources in the setting, might also be popular materials for use at home. By enabling the child to talk about nursery at home they have the additional virtue of linking home and school in quite explicit ways.

In some early years settings special classes have been set up so that parents can work together with a tutor to produce packs of materials designed to support parents' involvement in their children's mathematical development. The tutor is able to guide parents as to how and why particular resources will be helpful – thus furthering their understanding of the process. The Basic Skills Agency (www.basic-skills.co.uk) supports parents' understanding of their children's learning by focusing on the parents' own mathematical competence. The agency's current priorities include meeting the needs of young parents; the parents of children under the age of 3 and children who have little or no preschool experience.

Merttens and Vass (1990) are of the view that parents should be encouraged to make written responses when they have used mathematics materials at home. Early childhood educators will want to consider the extent to which they feel this is worthwhile. There is an opportunity for conversation with a child's parent or carer on most days, and these chats, sometimes very informal, can be invaluable. Demands for written responses may disadvantage parents who cannot read or write English or who do not find writing easy. However, a written record as an addition to regular face-to-face discussion has some merits. First, it invites the involvement of any parents who are not able to meet staff regularly. Second, it establishes a habit of written response which can be supportive as the child moves through primary schooling, where staff may see less of parents and may need mechanisms to keep in touch with parents. Some early years settings have resolved the issue by producing sheets which have columns with easily understood symbols which can be ticked or coloured, and may even be completed by the child with the support of the parent. A space may be added for those parents who wish to add a written comment.

If the staff of a particular setting feel that written responses would be useful they will need to design a format with which parents will feel comfortable. In nurseries which are separate from primary schools, it may be useful to make contact in order to make some link between approaches adopted in the early years setting and those which will be adopted in the primary school. If more elaborate responses are sought, schools with bilingual populations may need to translate forms into relevant languages. They may also need to consider how monolingual staff can gain insight into parents' views.

Atkinson (1992: 23) describes 'helping children to make the links between home and school maths' as 'a vital and important task for teachers and parents in the maths education of children'. The younger the child the more this responsibility can realistically *only* be carried by the adults who have responsibility for their care and education. As children grow older, they may share in the task of linking home and school, but neither parents nor professionals should allow this to become a burden to the child which it will do if disagreement or conflict cloud the relationship (Jowett 1991). The Rumbold Report (DES 1990: para. 100) summarizes the role which professionals must take on:

> They need to be able to share responsibility with parents. This places considerable demands upon the educators: they need to be ready to spend time on it, and to exercise sensitivity; they also need to have enough confidence to invite parents to share in their children's education.

Furthermore, within the partnership, professionals must take responsibility for ensuring that parents understand why this sharing is so vital to each child's future mathematical development and what role each of the partners can most helpfully play. Only by being fully aware of the child's total experience can parents and educators effectively challenge children's mathematical thinking. Table 6.1 outlines aspects of partnership which can be developed in supporting children's mathematical learning and thinking.

Table 6.1 Ways in which partnership with parents can support mathematical development

Parents as partners (QCA 2000: 9–10)	Partnership strategies to support mathematical development
Practitioners show respect and understanding for the role of the parent in their child's education.	Staff develop strategies to increase confidence in their ability to do and enjoy mathematics.
The past and future part played by parents in the education of their children is recognized and explicitly encouraged.	Staff need to work with parents on understanding the long-term consequences of the way in which children develop mathematically. There may be life-long consequences if children develop negative dispositions towards mathematics or if their confidence is undermined.
Practitioners listen to parents' accounts of the child's development and any concerns they have.	Opportunities for parents to meet staff (formally or informally) and to contribute to assessments or records need to address mathematical development as well as other aspects of the curriculum.
Arrangements for settling-in are flexible enough to give time for children to become secure and for practitioners and parents to discuss each child's circumstances, interests, skills and needs.	Parents' insight into children's persistent concerns and to the mathematical experiences that they have can help staff to plan appropriate learning and stimulating mathematical opportunities.
All parents are made to feel welcome, valued and necessary through a range of different opportunities for collaboration between children, parents and practitioners. The knowledge and expertise of parents and other family adults are used to support the learning opportunities provided by the setting.	Basic Skills Agency classes Devising and making mathematics packs for use at home Inviting parents in to talk about their work, or cook, garden etc., demonstrating mathematical expertise Curriculum evenings where a range of mathematical experiences are demonstrated in the setting for parents to explore Books and/or CDs of mathematical songs and rhymes to sing at home

Table 6.1 (*continued*)

Parents as partners (QCA 2000: 9–10)	Partnership strategies to support mathematical development
Practitioners use a variety of ways to keep parents fully informed about the curriculum, such as the brochures, displays and videos which are available in the home languages of the parent and though informal discussion.	Leaflets, displays and videos (either commercial ones aimed at parents or ones made by the staff featuring children in the setting) can help parents to see the range of possibilities for exciting mathematical experiences
Parents and practitioners talk about and record information about the child's progress and achievements, for example through meetings or making a book about the child.	Profile books used in many early years settings to highlight children's experiences can give parents an insight into the mathematics that children are engaged in.
Relevant learning activities and play activities, such as reading and sharing books are continued at home. Similarly, experiences at home are used to develop learning in the setting, for example visits and celebrations.	Staff might need to talk to parents about suitable ways of celebrating and the ways in which mathematics can be brought into the event. Parental help will be needed for visits and this is an excellent way to share expertise.

Summary

The difficulties of maintaining a partnership between parents and professionals are heightened in relation to mathematics since parents often have fixed ideas about what counts as maths and professionals are often insecure and defensive about their own understanding of the subject. As professionals, early years carers and educators must, for the sake of the child's development, take a lead in involving parents. This will include a wide range of strategies – explaining, sharing planning and records, discussing, encouraging parents to play mathematical games and sing rhymes – in fact anything which will bring home and institutional settings closer and bridge the differences for the child.

Conclusion

We need to help young children not to 'do' maths, but to use those mathematical tools created by the people of many cultures and centuries in order to recreate mathematics in their world and in this way to become young mathematicians.

(Metz 1987: 201)

No one could deny that something is going wrong somewhere with mathematics education in Britain. Yet, as we have seen, young children are immensely competent. Something prevents many of them from achieving in later years the promise they showed as young children. The drive and determination which they show as young learners is rarely translated into enthusiasm for learning mathematics in primary and secondary schools. Hughes (1986a: 184) refers to this phenomenon as a challenge:

We have on our side . . . a strength which is often underestimated: the immense capacity of young children to grasp difficult ideas if they are presented in ways which interest them and make sense to them. It is not always easy to design situations which meet these criteria but . . . the attempt to do so is usually worthwhile. If we can redesign our educational environments . . . so that, instead of nullifying and ignoring young children's strengths, we are able to bring them into play and build on them, then I am confident that we will be able to meet the challenge currently facing us.

Politicians, employers and educationalists whose main expertise lies in subjects of the curriculum or in working with older students may be sceptical about young children's strengths. However, parents and primary carers who are the experts on their own child's learning and early childhood specialists who have insight into young children's learning in general do not doubt it. We must therefore work together, in partnership, to convince everyone that we have answers to some of the dilemmas facing us.

The first task before early childhood practitioners is to convince ourselves that we have something to say which needs to be heard. The insights of the pioneers of early childhood education in Britain were based on observation. Their central tenets in relation to social interaction, the role of dialogue and the fundamental importance of physical thought in action are increasingly supported by research findings. These insights are crucial to our understanding of development, including the development of mathematical thinking. A developmentally appropriate curriculum, with its emphases on respect for children's individuality, on the need to engage with each child's individual starting point for learning, and the vital involvement of parents in ensuring coherent experiences (Hurst and Joseph 1998), builds on these insights.

Also crucial is the early childhood practice of interactive teaching – building on what children know and can do in order to help them learn more. Currently, external bodies are placing an emphasis on the curriculum map – the early learning goals, the National Numeracy Strategy and the National Curriculum all tell us where children must get to. This information is only useful if we are clear about where children are starting from and what interests and understandings are driving them. A railway map is of no value if you're travelling on a bicycle. It is important to know the destination but those who have defined it must remember two things. First, there are many routes – children's mathematical learning is not a ladder but more closely resembles a jigsaw. Second, children have to undertake the journey for themselves. Learning, including mathematical learning, is an active process and although adults may direct, instruct, cajole, demand, model, tell and ask, in the end the child is the one who determines what is learnt. This is in no way to suggest that adults do not have a crucial role to play in that learning process. But the support or scaffolding which they offer will be most effective when placed along the child's chosen route. Practitioners must observe, plan and implement a supportive approach which they think will help the child and then evaluate the extent to which it is helping learning.

At the same time, early childhood practitioners will also have to become more confident about their own mathematical abilities, since it is often insecurity which leads staff to fall back on the ways in which they were (often largely unsuccessfully) taught mathematics. This will involve inservice education, mutual support and learning alongside the children. It is increasingly evident that we all get better at doing things by doing them. It may also be, however, that we must learn to work in partnership with experts in mathematics. They may be surprised to find that they can learn from those who work with young children. Professor Shayer of King's College for example is quoted as saying:

> We are moving towards a different way of teaching, not just of maths and science but of everything – one that is not just concerned with kids' conceptual knowledge but with the quality of their underlying thinking.
>
> (Barnard 1997: 4)

Independence and discussion are seen as fundamental to the approach which he is advocating to science education. There is also an emphasis on helping children to think about how they learn. The legacy of the early childhood pioneers and the insights of early childhood practitioners will yet be vindicated!

Instruction has a role to play in learning but it cannot successfully operate outside the young child's concerns. The most skilful teachers of young children seize their opportunities, creating and exploiting the teachable moments. In this they have learnt from the intuitive teaching which occurs between parents and children in the home.

Vicky Hurst (1987: 109) has described parents' involvement in the education of their school-age children as 'the greatest single opportunity for educational advance'. Their involvement before and at the start of statutory schooling has even more potential. In relation to mathematics, the opportunities are immense. Working in partnership with parents, professionals can learn more about the children they teach and more about how they have learnt all that they know when they enter an early years setting. Parents can learn from professionals more about what counts as mathematics and why.

Learning to think mathematically is within the grasp of all. Those who have the privilege of working with young children and their families are part of the solution to the problem. We must, as did the pioneers of early childhood education, trust our insights and intuitions. However, we must also make our voices heard – thinking mathematically involves much more than mathematics. It depends upon a playful, reflective and respected start to learning.

References

Alexander, R. (1997) 'Basics, cores, margins and choices: towards a new primary curriculum', in *Developing the Primary School Curriculum: the Next Steps*. A collection of papers from an invitational conference held by the School Curriculum and Assessment Authority, 9–10 June. London: SCAA.

Anghileri, J. (ed.) (1995) *Children's Mathematical Thinking in the Primary Years*. London: Cassell.

Athey, C. (1990) *Extending Thought in Young Children*. London: Paul Chapman.

Atkinson, S. (ed.) (1992) *Mathematics with Reason: the Emergent Approach to Primary Maths*. London: Hodder and Stoughton.

Atkinson, S. and Clarke, S. (1992a) 'The use of standard notation', in S. Atkinson (ed.) *Mathematics with Reason*. London: Hodder and Stoughton.

Atkinson, S. and Clarke, S. (1992b) 'Children's own mathematical representations', in S. Atkinson (ed.) *Mathematics with Reason*. London: Hodder and Stoughton.

Atkinson, T. and Claxton, G. (2000) *The Intuitive Practitioner*. Buckingham: Open University Press.

Aubrey, C. (ed.) (1994) *The Role of Subject Knowledge in the Early Years of Schooling*. London: Falmer Press.

Baker, L. (1995) 'Re-solving problem-solving', in Anghileri, J. (ed.) *Children's Mathematical Thinking in the Primary Years*. London: Cassell.

Ball, C. (1994) *Start Right: The Importance of Early Learning*. London: RSA.

Barnard, N. (1997) 'A learning revolution spreads', *Times Educational Supplement*, 17 October.

BEAM (2003) *Starting Out – Foundation Stage Mathematics*. London: BEAM Education.

Blakemore, S-J. and Frith, U. (2005) *The Learning Brain – Lessons For Education*. Oxford: Blackwell Publishing.

Bresler, L. (ed.) (2004) *Knowing Bodies, Moving Minds.* London: Kluwer Academic Publishers.

Bronfenbrenner, U. (1979) *The Ecology of Human Development.* London: Harvard University Press.

Brown, T. (1996) 'Play and number', in R. Merttens, (ed.) *Teaching Numeracy.* Leamington Spa: Scholastic Press.

Browne, E. (1995) *Handa's Surprise.* London: Walker Paperbacks.

Browne, N. (ed.) (1991) *Science and Technology in the Early Years.* Buckingham: Open University Press.

Bruce, T. (1991) *Time to Play in Early Childhood Education.* London: Hodder and Stoughton.

Bruce, T. (2005a) (3rd edn) *Early Childhood Education.* London: Hodder Arnold.

Bruce, T. (2005b) (2nd edn) 'Play, the universe and everything!' in J. Moyles (ed.) *The Excellence of Play.* Maidenhead: Open University Press.

Bruner, J. (1983) *Child's Talk.* New York: Norton.

Bruner, J. (1986) *Actual Minds: Possible Worlds.* London: Harvard University Press.

Bruner, J. and Haste, H. (1987) *Making Sense – the Child's Construction of the World.* London: Methuen.

Bryant, P. (1997) 'Mathematical understanding in the nursery school years', in T. Nunes and P. Bryant (eds) *Learning and Teaching Mathematics: an International Perspective.* Hove, East Sussex: Psychology Press.

Buck, L. (1996) *The Pound Park Experience.* London: Greenwich Education Service.

Burningham, J. (1972) *Mr. Gumpy's Outing.* London: Jonathan Cape.

Burton, L. (1994) *Children Learning Mathematics: Patterns and Relationships.* Hemel Hempstead: Simon and Schuster Education.

Butterworth, B. (1999) *The Mathematical Brain.* London: Macmillan.

Butterworth, B. (2005) 'The development of arithmetical abilities', *Journal of Child Psychology and Psychiatry* 46: 1003–18.

Carle, E. (1969) *The Very Hungry Caterpillar.* London: Hamish Hamilton.

Carr, M. (1992) *Maths for Meaning: Tracing a Path for Early Mathematical Development.* Hamilton, New Zealand: University of Waikato Centre for Science and Mathematics Research.

Carr, M. (2001) *Assessment in Early Childhood – Learning Stories.* London: Paul Chapman.

Carraher, T. N., Carraher, D. W. and Schliemann, A. D. (1991) 'Mathematics in the streets and in schools', in P. Light, S. Sheldon and M. Woodhead (eds) *Learning to Think.* London: Routledge.

Carter, R. (1999) *Mapping the Mind.* London: Seven Dials.

Chiu, C., Hong, Y. and Dweck, C. (1994) 'Towards an integrative model of personality and intelligence: a general framework and some preliminary steps', in R. J. Sternberg and P. Ruxgis (eds) *Personality and Intelligence.* Cambridge: Cambridge University Press.

City of Westminster (not dated) *Great Expectations.* London: City of Westminster Education Department.

Clarke, S. and Atkinson, S. (1996) *Tracking Significant Achievement in Primary Mathematics*. London: Hodder and Stoughton.

Claxton, G. (1997) *Hare Brain and Tortoise Mind*. London: Fourth Estate.

Claxton, G. (2000) 'The anatomy of intuition', in T. Atkinson and G. Claxton (eds) *The Intuitive Practitioner: on the Value of not Always Knowing what One is Doing*. Buckingham: Open University Press.

Clements, D. H. and Sarama, J. (eds) (2004) *Engaging Young Children in Mathematics*. London: Lawrence Erlbaum Associates.

Clemson, D. and Clemson, W. (1994) *Mathematics in the Early Years*. London: Routledge.

Copple, C. E. (2004) 'Mathematics Curriculum in the Early Childhood Context', in D. H. Clements and J. Sarama (eds) *Engaging Young Children in Mathematics*. London: Lawrence Erlbaum Associates.

Cousins, J. (1990) Are your little Humpty Dumpties floating or sinking? *Early Years*, 10(2): 23–38.

Cox, T. and Sanders, S. (1994) *The Impact of the National Curriculum on the Teaching of Five Year Olds*. London: Falmer Press.

Craft, A. (2001) 'Little c Creativity', in A. Craft, B. Jeffrey and M. Leibling (eds) *Creativity in Education*. London: Continuum.

David, T. (1992) What do parents want their children to learn in pre-school in Belgium and the UK? Paper presented at the XXth World Congress of OMEP, North Arizona University, Flagstaff, Ariz.

Davies, M. (1995) *Helping Children to Learn through a Movement Perspective*. London: Hodder and Stoughton.

Davis, J. H. (1997) 'The What and the Whether of the U: Cultural Implications of Understanding Development in Graphic Symbolization', *Human Development* 40: 145–54.

Dehaene, S. (1997) *The Number Sense*. London: Penguin Group.

DES (Department of Education and Science) (1982) *Mathematics Counts* (Cockcroft Report). London: HMSO.

DES (Department of Education and Science) (1990) *Starting with Quality*. (Rumbold Report). London: HMSO.

Devi, S. (1990) *Figuring*. London: Penguin

Devlin, K. (2000) *The Maths Gene*. London: Weidenfeld and Nicolson.

DfEE (Department for Education and Employment) (1998) *The National Literacy Strategy*. Sudbury, Suffolk: DfEE Publications.

DfEE (Department for Education and Employment) (1999) *The National Numeracy Strategy*. Sudbury, Suffolk: DfEE Publications.

DfES (Department for Education and Skills) (2002) *Mathematical Activities for the Foundation Stage: Introductory Pack*. London: DFES/NNS.

DfES (Department for Education and Skills) (2003) *Excellence and Enjoyment – a Strategy for Primary Schools*. London: DFES.

Doherty, J. and Bailey, R. (2003) *Supporting Physical Development and Physical Education in the Early Years*. Buckingham: Open University Press.

Doman, G. and Doman, J. (1994) *How to Teach your Baby Math*. New York: Avery Publishing Group.

Donaldson, M. (1976) *Children's Minds*. London: Fontana.

Donaldson, M. (1992) *Human Minds*. Harmondsworth: Penguin.

Donaldson, M. (1986) *Children's Minds*. London: Fontana.

Dowling, M. (2005) (2nd edn) *Young Children's Personal, Social and Emotional Development*. London: Paul Chapman.

Duffy, B. (1998) *Supporting Creativity and Imagination in the Early Years*. Buckingham: Open University Press.

Dunn, J. (1988) *The Beginnings of Social Understanding*. Oxford: Blackwell.

Durkin, D. (2001) *Thinking Together: quality adult children interactions*. Wellington: New Zealand Council for Educational Research.

Edgington, M. (2004) (3rd edn) *The Foundation Stage Teacher in Action*. London: Paul Chapman.

Edgington, M., Fisher, J., Morgan, M., Pound, L. and Scott, W. (1998) *Interpreting the National Curriculum*. Buckingham: Open University Press.

Egan, K. (1988) *Primary Understanding*. London: Routledge.

Egan, K. (1989) *Teaching as Storytelling*. London: Routledge.

Eliot, L. (1999) *Early Intelligence*. London: Penguin.

Fisher, J. (2002) *Starting from the Child*. Buckingham: Open University Press.

Gardner, H. (1993) *The Unschooled Mind*. London: Fontana.

Gardner, H. (1999) *Intelligence Reframed*. New York: Basic Books.

Gerhardt, S. (2004) *Why Love Matters*. Hove: Brunner-Routledge.

Gifford, S. (1995) 'Number in Early Childhood', *Early Childhood Development and Care* 109: 95–119

Gifford, S. (2005a) *Young Children's Difficulties in Learning Mathematics*. London: QCA.

Gifford, S. (2005b) *Teaching Mathematics 3–5: Developing Learning in the Foundation Stage*. Maidenhead: Open University Press.

Ginsburg, H., Choy, Y. E., Lopez, L. S., Netley, R. and Chao-Yuan, C. (1997) 'Happy Birthday to you: early mathematical thinking of Asian, South American and US children', in T. Nunes and P. Bryant (eds) *Learning and Teaching Mathematics: an International Perspective*. Hove, East Sussex: Psychology Press.

Goldschmied, E. (1990) *Heuristic Play with Objects, and Infants learning*. London: National Children's Bureau.

Goldschmied, E. and Selleck, D. (1996) *Communication between Babies in their First Year* (video). London: National Children's Bureau.

Goleman, D. (1996) *Emotional Intelligence*. London: Fontana.

Gopnik, A., Meltzoff, A. and Kuhl, P. (1999) *How Babies Think*. London: Weidenfeld and Nicolson.

Greenfield, S. (1996) *The Human Mind Explained*. London: Cassell.

Griffiths, R. (2005) 'Mathematics and play', in J. Moyles (ed.) *The Excellence of Play*. Maidenhead: Open University Press.

Gura, P. (ed.) (1992) *Exploring Learning: Young Children and Block Play*. London: Paul Chapman.

Hall, N., Gillen, J. and Greenhall, R. (1996) '"Don't Cry, I ring the cop shop": young children's pretend telephone behaviours', in N. Hall and J. Martello (eds) *Listening to Children Think: Exploring Talk in the Early Years.* London: Hodder and Stoughton.

Harrison, C. and Pound, L. (1996) 'Talking music: empowering children as musical communicators', *British Journal of Music Education*, 13: 233–42.

Healy, J. (1999) *Failure to Connect.* New York: Touchstone.

Hughes, M. (1986a) *Children and Number.* Oxford: Basil Blackwell.

Hughes, M. (1986b) 'Young children learning in the community', in *Involving Parents in the Primary Curriculum.* Exeter: University of Exeter.

Hurst, V. (1987) 'Parents and professionals: partnerships in early childhood education', in G. Blenkin and A. V. Kelly (eds) *Early Childhood Education: A Developmental Curriculum.* London: Paul Chapman.

Hurst, V. and Joseph, J. (1998) *Supporting Early Learning: The Way Forward.* Buckingham: Open University Press.

Hutchin, V. (1996) *Tracking Significant Achievement in the Early Years.* London: Hodder and Stoughton.

Hutchins, P. (1968) *Rosie's Walk.* London: Bodley Head.

Hutchins, P. (1986) *The Doorbell Rang.* London: Bodley Head.

Jenkinson, S. (2001) *The Genius of Play.* Stroud, Glos: Hawthorn Press.

Jowett, S. (1991) *Building Bridges: Parental Involvement in Schools.* Windsor, Berks: NFER-Nelson.

Karmiloff, K. and Karmiloff-Smith, A. (2001) *Pathways to Language.* London: Harvard University Press.

Karmiloff-Smith, A. (1994) *Baby it's You.* London: Bodley Head.

Kelly, A. V. (1994) 'Beyond the rhetoric and the discourse', in G. Blenkin and A. V. Kelly (eds) *The National Curriculum and Early Learning.* London: Paul Chapman.

Kerslake, D., Burton, L., Harvey, R., Street, L. and Walsh, A. (1990) *HBJ Mathematics: Teacher's Resource Book.* London: Harcourt Brace Jovanovich.

Lally, M. (1991) *The Nursery Teacher in Action.* London: Paul Chapman.

Lee, T. and Tompsett, I. (2004) *Dramatic Mathematics.* London: MakeBelieve Arts.

Lewis, A. (1996) *Discovering Mathematics with 4- to 7-year olds.* London: Hodder and Stoughton.

London Borough of Lewisham (not dated) *Continuity Counts – Guidance on Effective Practice in Year 1.* London: London Borough of Lewisham

Lucas, B. (2001) *Power up your Mind.* London: Nicholas Brealey Publishing.

MacGregor, H. (1998) *Tom Thumb's Musical Maths.* London: A&C Black.

Macnamara, A. (1996) 'From home to school – do children preserve their counting skills?', in P. Broadhead (ed.) *Researching the Early Years Continuum.* Clevedon: Multilingual Matters.

Malaguzzi, L. (1995) 'History, ideas and basic philosophy', in C. Edwards, L. Gandini and G. Forman (eds) *The Hundred Languages of Children.* Norwoord, New Jersey: Ablex Publishing Corporation.

Malaguzzi, L. (1997) *Shoe and Meter*. Municipality of Reggio Emilia: Reggio Children.

Manning-Morton, J. and Thorp, M. (2001) *Key Times: a Framework for Developing High Quality Provision for Children under Three Years*. London: Camden EYDCP/ University of North London.

Manning-Morton, J. and Thorp, M. (2003) *Key Times for Play*. Maidenhead: Open University Press.

Marsden, L. and Woodbridge, J. (2005) *Looking Closely at Learning and Teaching... a journey of development*. Huddersfield: Early Excellence Ltd.

Matthews, J. (2003) (2nd edn) *Drawing and Painting: Children and Visual Representation*. London: Paul Chapman.

Mazur, B. (2003) *Imagining Numbers*. London: Penguin.

McMillan, M. (1930) *The Nursery School*. London: Dent.

Meek, M. (1982) *Learning to Read*. London: Bodley Head.

Meek, M. (1985) 'Play and paradoxes: some consideration of imagination and language', in G. Wells and J. Nicholls (eds) *Language and Learning: an Interactional Perspective*. London: Falmer Press.

Menmuir, J. and Adams, K. (1997) 'Young children's inquiry learning in mathematics' *Early Years* 17(2): 34–9.

Merttens, R. (1996) *Teaching Numeracy: Maths in the Primary Classroom*. Leamington Spa: Scholastic Press.

Merttens, R. (1997) 'Chants would be a fine thing', *Times Educational Supplement* 24 January.

Merttens, R. and Vass, J. (1990) *Sharing Maths Cultures*. Basingstoke: Falmer Press.

Metz, M. (1987) 'The development of mathematical understanding', in G. Blenkin and A. V. Kelly (eds) *The National Curriculum and Early Learning*. London: Paul Chapman.

Ministry of Education (1996) *Te Whariki He Whaariki Matauranga: Early Childhood Curriculum*. Wellington, New Zealand: Learning Media.

Mithen, S. (1996) *The Prehistory of the Mind*. London: Thames and Hudson.

Mithen, S. (2005) *The Singing Neanderthals*. London: Weidenfeld and Nicolson.

Montague-Smith, A. (2002) (2nd edn) *Mathematics in Nursery Education*. London: David Fulton.

Montessori, M. (1912) *The Montessori Method*. London: Heinemann.

Moore, I. (2004) *Six Dinner Sid*. London: Hodder.

Moyles, J. (1994) *The Excellence of Play*. Buckingham: Open University Press.

Munn, P. (1994) Counter intelligence at work. *Times Educational Supplement*, 5 April.

Munn, P. and Schaffer, H. R. (1993) 'Literacy and numeracy events in social interactive contexts', *International Journal of Early Years Education*, 1(3): 61–80.

Murray, L. and Andrews, L. (2000) *The Social Baby*. Richmond, Surrey: CP Publishing.

NNP (National Numeracy Project) (1997) *Hungarian Primary Mathematics Classes*. NNP video.

Nunes, T. (1996) Learning mathematics in primary school: from informal to formal. Susan Isaacs lecture, presented to the University of London Institute of Education, 16 November.

Nutbrown, C. (1999) (2nd edn) *Threads of Thinking*. London: Paul Chapman.

Odam, G. (1995) *The Sounding Symbol*. Cheltenham: Stanley Thornes.

Owen, A. and Rousham, L. (1997) 'Maths – is that a kind of game for grown-ups? Understanding numbers in the early years', in D. Whitebread (ed.) *Teaching and Learning in the Early Years*. London: Routledge.

Paley, V. G. (1981) *Wally's Stories*. Cambridge, Mass: Harvard University Press.

Paley, V. G. (1988) *Bad Guys Don't Have Birthdays*. Chicago: University of Chicago Press.

Paley, V. G. (1990) *The Boy Who Would Be a Helicopter*. Cambridge, Mass: Harvard University Press.

Papert, S. (1982) *Mindstorms*. Brighton: Harvester Press.

Papousek, H. (1994) 'To the evolution of human musicality and musical education', in I. Deliege (ed.) *Proceedings of the 3rd International Conference for Music Perception and Cognition*. Liege: ESCOM.

Papousek, H. and Papousek, M. (1987) 'Intuitive parenting', in J. D. Oakley (ed.) *Handbook of Infant Development*. New York: Wiley.

Parkin, R. (1991) 'Fair play: children's mathematical experiences in the infant classroom', in N. Browne (ed.) *Science and Technology in the Early Years*. Buckingham: Open University Press.

Phillips, A. (1998) *The Beast in the Nursery*. London: Faber and Faber.

Pound, L. (2004) 'Born mathematical?' in L. Miller and J. Devereux (eds) *Supporting Children's Learning in the Early Years*. London: David Fulton.

Pound, L. (2005) *How Children Learn*. Leamington Spa: Step Forward Publishing.

Pound, L. and Gura, P. (1997) 'Communities of experts', in P. Gura (ed.) *Reflections on Early Education and Care*. London: British Association for Early Childhood Education.

Pound, L. and Harrison, C. (2003) *Supporting Musical Development in the Early Years*. Buckingham: Open University Press.

Pound, L., Cook, L., Court, J., Stevenson, J. and Wadsworth, J. (1992) *The Early Years: Mathematics*. London: Harcourt Brace Jovanovich.

Pugh, G. and De'ath, E. (1984) *The Needs of Parents*. London: Macmillan.

QCA (Qualification and Assessment Authority) (1999) *The National Curriculum for England*. London: DfEE/QCA.

QCA (Qualification and Assessment Authority) (2000) *Curriculum Guidance for the Foundation Stage*. London: DfEE/QCA.

QCA/DfES (2003) *Foundation Stage Profile Handbook*. London: QCA.

Ramachandran, V. S. (2004) *A Brief History of Human Consciousness*. London: BBC/Profile Books.

Ramachandran, V. S. and Blakeslee, S. (1999) *Phantoms in the Brain*. London: Fourth Estate.

Rinaldi, C. (1997) 'A measure for friendship', in M. Castagnetti and V. Vecchi (eds) *Shoe and Meter*. Municipality of Reggio Emilia: Regio Children.

Rogers, J. (1997) 'Shopping around for answers', *Times Educational Supplement*, 11 July.

Rogoff, B. (1990) *Apprenticeship in Thinking*. Oxford: Oxford University Press.

Rogoff, B. (2003) *The Cultural Nature of Human Development*. Oxford: Oxford University Press.

Ross, T. (2003) *Centipede's 100 Shoes*. London: Andersen Press.

Sammons, P., Sylva, K., Melhuish, E., Siraj-Blatchford, I., Taggart, B. and Elliot, K. (2002) *Measuring the Impact of pre-school on children's cognitive progress over the pre-school period*. London: Institute of Education/DfES.

Sayre, A. and Sayre, J. (2004) *One is a Snail, Ten is a Crab*. London: Walker Books.

Schiro, M. S. (2004) *Oral Storytelling and Teaching Mathematics*. London: Sage.

Selleck, D. (1997) 'Baby art: art is me', in P. Gura (ed.) *Reflections on Early Education and Care*. London: British Association for Early Childhood Education.

Seo, K-H. and Ginsburg, H. (2004) 'What is developmentally appropriate in early childhood mathematics education? Lessons from new research', in D. H. Clements and J. Sarama (eds) *Engaging Young Children in Mathematics*. London: Lawrence Erlbaum Associates.

Siegel, D. (1999) *The Developing Mind*. New York: Guilford Press.

Sinclair, A. (1988) 'La notation numérique chez l'enfant', in H. Sinclair (ed.) *La production de notations chez le jeune enfant: langage, nombre, rythmes et mélodies*. Paris: Presses Universitaires de France.

Siraj-Blatchford, I., Sylva, K., Muttock, S., Gilden, R. and Bell, D. (2002) *Researching Effective Pedagogy in the Early Years*. London: Institute of Education/ Department of Educational Studies, University of Oxford.

Skinner, C. and Ebbutt, S. (not dated) *Maths is Everywhere*. London: Early Education (Learning together series).

Skinner, C. (2005) *Maths Outdoors*. London: BEAM Education.

Steffe, L. (2004) 'PSSM (Principles and Standards for School Mathematics) from a constructivist perspective', in D. H. Clements and J. Sarama (eds) *Engaging Young Children in Mathematics*. London: Lawrence Erlbaum Associates.

Stobbs, W. (1968) *The Story of the Three Little Pigs*. Harmondsworth: Penguin.

Sure Start Unit (2002) *Birth to Three Matters*. London: DfES.

Sylva, K. (1997) 'The early years curriculum, evidence based proposals', in *Developing the Primary School Curriculum: the next steps*. A collection of papers from an invitational conference held by the School Curriculum and Assessment Authority, 9–10 June. London: SCAA.

Tacon, R. and Atkinson, R. (1997) *Teaching Infants Mental Arithmetic*. Peacehaven County Infants School (pamphlet).

Thumpston, G. (1994) 'Mathematics in the National Curriculum: implications for learning in the early years', in G. Blenkin and A. V. Kelly (eds) *The National Curriculum and Early Learning*. London: Paul Chapman.

Tizard, B. and Hughes, M. (1984) *Young Children Learning*. London: Fontana.

Tizard, B., Blatchford, P., Burke, J., Farquhar, C. and Plewis, I. (1988) *Young Children at School in the Inner City*. Hove, East Sussex: Lawrence Erlbaum Associates.

Tizard, B. and Hughes, M. (1984) *Young Children Learning*. London: Fontana.

Tobin, J. (2004) 'The disappearance of the body in early childhood education', in L. Bresler (ed.) *Knowing Bodies, Moving Minds*. London: Kluwer Academic Publishers.

Trevarthen, C. (1990) 'Signs before speech', in T. A. Sebeok and J. U. Sebeok (eds) *The Semiotic Web*. Berlin: Mouton de Gruyter.

Trevarthen, C. (1998) 'The child's need to learn a culture', in M. Woodhead, D. Faulkner and K. Littleton (eds) *Cultural Worlds of Early Childhood*. London: Routledge.

Tucker, K. (2005) *Mathematics through Play in the Early Years*. London: Paul Chapman.

Vygotsky, L. S. (1978) *Mind in Society*. Cambridge, Mass: Harvard University Press.

Vygotsky, L. S. (1986) *Thought and Language*. Cambridge, Mass: MIT Press.

Walkerdine, V. (1988) *The Mastery of Reason*. London: Routledge.

Walkerdine, V. (1989) *Counting Girls Out*. London: Virago.

Walsh, D. (2004) 'Frog boy and the American monkey: the body in Japanese early schooling', in L. Bresler (ed.) *Knowing Bodies, Moving Minds*. London: Kluwer Academic Publishers.

Wells, G. (1985) *Language Development in the Preschool Years*. Cambridge: Cambridge University Press.

Whalley, M. (1994) *Learning to be Strong*. Sevenoaks: Hodder and Stoughton.

Whitin, D. J. and Wilde, S. (1995) *It's the Story that Counts*. Portsmouth: Heinemann.

Widlake, P. and Macleod, F. (1984) *Raising Standards*. Coventry: Community Education Development Centre.

Williams, H. (1996) 'Developing numeracy in the early years', in R. Merttens (ed.) *Teaching Numeracy*. Leamington Spa: Scholastic Press.

Womack, D. (1993) 'Game, set and match?', *Times Educational Supplement*, 8 October.

Wood, D. (1991) 'Aspects of teaching and learning', in P.Light, S. Sheldon and M. Woodhead (eds) *Learning to think*. London: Routledge.

Worthington, M. and Carruthers, E. (2003) *Children's Mathematics: making marks, making meaning*. London: Paul Chapman.

Young-Loveridge, J. M. (1987) 'Learning mathematics', *British Journal of Developmental Psychology*, 5: 155–67.

Young-Loveridge, J. M. (1989) 'The relationship between children's home experiences and their mathematical skills on entry to school', *Early Child Development and Care*, 43: 43–59.

Index

abstract thought, 2, 3, 26, 27, 28, 33, 34–5, 40, 50, 54, 59, 68, 81, 86, 89, 92, 99, 102, 104, 113
activities, 123
  adult-directed, 88, 90, 112
  child-initiated, 84, 88–9
adult roles, 3, 45, 69, 72, 107, 11, 133
approximation, 12, 59, 67
  see also estimating, guessing,
area, 14, 40, 58
Athey, C., 3, 10, 35, 36, 62, 120
Atkinson, R., 24, 42, 72, 74, 142, 144, 145, 148
attitudes to mathematics, 5, 21–2, 46, 95
  see also dispositions
Aubrey, C., 47, 70, 125, 133

babies, 6–11, 21, 32, 35, 45, 51, 54, 58, 63, 94, 106, 107, 108, 118, 136, 138
Birth to Three Matters, 59, 62, 108–110
blockplay, 47, 85, 96, 133, 137
brain, 2, 8, 26, 32–3, 41, 42, 46, 51, 54, 66, 98, 120
Bruce, T., 50, 88, 124
Bruner, J,. 26, 27, 136
Bryant, P., 43, 56

Burton, L. 62, 12, 145
Butterworth, 7, 8, 55

calculation, *see* computation
capacity, 57, 99
Carr, M., 18, 59, 60–61
Clarke, S., 6, 23, 132
Claxton, G., 25, 28, 31, 42, 47, 48, 51, 66, 115, 120
Clemson, D. 47, 50, 114, 142
Cockroft Report, 1, 5, 144
communication, 5, 22, 26, 60–1, 83, 94, 106, 116, 145–8
communication, language and literacy, 102–5
comparison, 27, 37
computation, 2, 4, 16, 19, 23, 52, 77, 79, 93, 103
computers, *see* ICT
confidence, 4
  children's, 5, 6, 55, 59, 60, 65–66, 73, 103, 104, 110, 127
  parents' 142
  teachers'/practitioners', 2, 3, 24, 49, 65, 92, 117, 125, 128, 142, 152
connections, *see* making connections

continuity, 82, 98
cooking, 17, 88, 99, 101, 103, 131, 143
counting, 7, 12, 13, 30, 51, 55, 58, 69, 77, 78, 91, 99, 113137, 138–9,
    principles of, 53
    on, 19, 55, 90
    on fingers, 8, 14, 54, 69, 103
Creative approaches to mathematics, 101, 106
creative development, 102–5
creativity, 21, 42, 48, 65, 92, 110
culture, 6, 12, 18, 20, 22, 33, 44, 48, 58
curriculum, 51, 84, 91, 97, 125
    Curriculum Guidance for the Foundation Stage, see Foundation Stage; early learning goals
    developmentally appropriate curriculum, 71, 120, 124, 152
    mathematical content, 3, 50, 51, 56, 78–80, 84, 85–7, 126, 146
    mathematical processes, 3, 43, 50, 81, 85–7
    see also National Curriculum; National Numeracy Strategy

dance, *see* music
developmental psychology, 2, 28
Devlin, K., 2, 3, 7, 28, 32, 33, 34–5, 54, 62, 66, 68
discussion, 24, 153
dispositions, 3, 5, 33, 46, 59–61, 102, 142–3
distance, 4, 9, 14, 38,44
documentation, 120
Dowling, M.,59, 60–1

EAL (English as an additional language), 45, 95, 132, 134, 135, 147
early learning goals, 31, 52, 65, 73, 97, 111, 117, 152
Edgington, M., 31, 68, 88, 125
Egan, K., 9, 71, 93, 106
emotions, 46, 48, 96, 100, 106, 109

enthusiasms, 35
    see also persistent concerns; interests; enthusiasms
errors, 22, 78, 132
estimating, 37, 58, 59, 67, 80, 99
evaluation, 121–2, 135
everyday experiences, 1, 2, 4, 17–8, 59, 70, 83, 122
exploration, 9, 14, 17, 18, 32, 34, 37, 38, 40, 59, 62, 84, 87, 97, 99, 100, 103, 106, 108–9

fast-mapping, 10
Fisher, J., 88, 95, 113
foundation stage, 2, 25, 31, 51, 52, 59, 62, 78, 111–4, 125
    profile, 125
Froebel, F., 56–7, 120, 124

games, 24, 72, 90–1, 96, 114, 116, 122, 143, 146, 150
    tins game, 74–5
Gardner, H., 9, 12, 18, 26, 27, 28, 36, 106
gender, 2, 57, 65–66, 122, 132, 134, 135, 142
Gerhardt, S., 106, 120
Gifford, S. 8, 16,19, 46, 58, 59, 63, 69, 74, 92, 93, 127, 130, 133, 143
Ginsburg, H., 43, 44
Goldschmeid, E., 25, 60
Gopnik, A., 7, 10, 11, 24, 64
Greenfield, S., 33, 48, 51, 120
guessing, 5, 8, 28, 55, 59, 66–7, 81, 85, 102, 113, 116
    see also approximation, estimating, hypothesising, predicting
Gura, P., 29, 76, 124, 125, 135

heuristic play, 108
Hill, L., 90, 96, 97, 129, 130, 132
home, 3, 11, 17, 22, 143
Hughes, M. 12, 14, 15, 16, 28, 30, 35, 69, 74, 75, 132, 135, 140, 151
humour, 24, 116

hundred languages of children, 25, 29
see also Malaguzzi, Reggio Emilia
hypothesising, 31, 67
see also approximation, estimating, guessing, predicting

ICT (information and communication technology), 3, 11, 15, 16, 36, 85, 86, 99, 100, 101, 103, 104, 122, 130, 135, 138–9
images, 16, 27, 68
imagination, 3, 27, 28, 32, 33, 34–5, 36, 65, 68–9, 70, 84, 90, 102, 104, 106, 109, 131
see also abstract thought
imitation, 32, 45
inclusion, 31,41,46, 95, 134–6
independence, 59, 64, 96, 128, 153
instruction, 108, 138
interests, 18, 35, 68, 83, 100, 107, 114, 133
see also persistent concerns
intervention, 133–6
see also adult-initiated activities, adult roles, questioning
intuition, 26, 28, 43, 65, 67
investigating, 87, 97, 113, 122, 129
Isaacs, S., 120

Karmiloff-Smith, A., 7, 32,
Key Stage 1, 51, 78, 98, 106, 114, 115
knowledge and understanding of the world, 52, 102–5

language, 3, 8, 10, 21, 22, 24, 25, 26, 43, 48, 56, 70, 71, 104, 108, 119
development, 21–4
positional 5, 58, 104
see also communication, language and literacy; EAL
learning, 6, 7, 10, 19, 21, 22, 28–9, 31, 32–3, 34–5, 42, 54, 59, 68–9, 71, 107, 112, 116
see also brain
length, 44, 57, 101, 121–2

Lewis, A., 1, 66, 69, 97, 126, 128, 132, 133, 134, 144
logic, 26, 28, 42, 67

MakeBelieve Arts, 101, 106
McGregor, H., 91, 116
McMillan, M., 42, 48, 112, 120
Macnamara, A., 19, 55, 143
making connections, 3, 31, 32, 33, 36, 39, 41–4, 45, 48, 51, 60, 62, 83, 96, 100–1, 109, 110, 114, 116, 128, 133
Malaguzzi, L. 17, 58, 106, 120
Manning-Morton, J., 37, 41, 101, 106
Marsden, L., 90, 91, 96, 97, 112, 122, 129
mass, 57
see also weight
mathematical development, 2, 22, 23, 102–5, 149–50

Matthews, J., 9, 10
Mazur, B., 33, 106
measurement, 4, 16, 52, 53, 56–8, 72, 78, 80, 104, 105, 113, 126
Menmuir, J., 36, 126, 128
mental images, 68, 74, 82
Merttens, R. 28, 31, 63, 64, 93, 106, 137, 138, 143, 147
Metz, M. 151
Mithen, S., 25, 26, 42
money, 44, 47, 55, 88, 89, 93, 135, 137, 143
Montague-Smith, A. 63, 112
Montessori, M. 45, 120
Moyles, J. 84, 88
Munn, P., 11, 23, 46, 59, 74
Murray, L., 32, 45
music, 8, 22, 27, 31, 54, 58, 91, 96, 104, 106, 112, 149

narrative, *see* stories
National Curriculum, 24, 25, 31, 97, 152
National Numeracy Strategy, 1, 2, 24, 25, 31, 45, 51, 52, 58, 65, 73, 77, 88, 114, 115, 117, 152

neuroscience, 2, 3, 33, 46, 56
  see also brain
number(s), 4, 11, 12, 15, 24, 52, 55, 69,
    77, 78, 85, 87, 93, 98, 103, 115,
    126–7, 130
  as labels, 4, 53
  cardinal, 52
  conservation, 12, 37
  large, 53, 54, 98, 99
  lines, 69, 115, 130
  notation, 14, 31, 73, 74
  operations 28 (see also
    computation)
  ordinal, 52
  square, 69, 85, 115
  system, 2, 54
numeracy, 1, 15
  see also National Numeracy
    Strategy
numerosity, 7, 8, 15, 55

observation, 3, 28, 97, 112, 118–23, 128,
    152
one-to-one correspondence, 14, 15, 16,
    40, 53, 90, 110
outdoors, 91, 101, 112, 130, 131

Paley, V. G., 16–17, 35, 43, 71, 91, 93, 96,
    106, 120
Papert, S., 36
Papousek, H., 65, 118, 139
parents, 6, 11, 26, 44, 49, 51, 63, 72, 119,
    122, 129, 133, 139, 140, 144, 149–50,
    153
  partnership with, 3, 140–4, 149–50,
    152
pattern, 2, 5, 7, 8, 9, 17–18, 28, 32, 37, 39,
    40, 51, 59, 62, 63, 64, 81, 85, 86, 104,
    113, 116, 123, 126, 131, 137
persistent concerns, 3, 35–41, 65, 96,
    101, 102, 153
  see also interests
physical activity, 10, 18, 25, 26, 27, 28,
    45, 58, 83, 101, 102, 104, 108, 117,
    123

physical development, 102–5
Piaget, J., 26, 27, 28, 63, 137
planning, 3, 119, 120, 122, 124, 125,
    126–8, 139, 150, 152
play, 3, 17, 18, 23, 27, 32, 33, 34–5, 36,
    41, 45, 47, 50, 51, 59, 68, 69, 70, 71,
    72, 74, 75, 82, 84, 88, 96, 97, 100,
    107, 108, 109, 112, 116, 118, 122,
    124, 131
  with language, 23
playfulness, 21, 24, 42, 47, 48, 65, 68, 83,
    84, 88, 90, 91, 92–3, 113, 115, 128,
    133, 153,
poetry of mathematics, 41, 42
Pound, L., 3, 8, 22, 41, 43, 46, 53, 54, 57,
    65, 91, 126
predicting, 67
  see also approximation, estimating,
    guessing, hypothesising
primary school, 24, 52, 55, 94, 114–6
problem-finding, 59, 60, 61, 64–6, 81,
    87, 102, 110, 113
problem-solving, 2, 5, 19, 50, 56, 61,
    64–6, 81, 82, 93, 96, 101, 104, 110,
    116, 129
props, 91, 92, 138, 146–7
  see also resources
PSE (personal, social and emotional
    development), 102–5
  see also emotions; independence;
    social interaction

quantity, 6, 14, 37, 38, 40
questioning, 34, 69, 93, 94, 96, 100, 133,
    134, 138, 142, 145

reception classes, 19, 30, 51, 62, 71, 108,
    112, 114, 125, 144
recording
  adults, 97, 121, 123–4, 129, 150
  children, 31, 71, 72, 74, 81, 82
  formal, 73, 125, 144
reflection, 43, 61, 96, 133
Reggio Emilia, 25, 26, 29, 120, 126
relevance, 24, 98–100

representation, 3, 8, 9, 12, 19, 25, 26, 29, 30, 31, 34–5, 36, 37, 57, 68, 72, 74, 75, 81, 96, 106, 110
resources, 12, 99, 107, 129–131, 133
    see also props, structured apparatus
rhymes, 17, 26, 45, 51, 53, 54, 63, 85, 91, 103,
risk-taking, 59, 102, 133
Rogoff, B., 58, 106
Rumbold Report, 144, 148

Sammons, P. 128, 146
schema, 37–40, 50, 63, 100
Schiro, M., 65, 67, 91, 92
Selleck, D. 9, 10
sensory experience, 25, 99, 109
shape and space, 4, 9, 24, 37, 38, 39, 40, 48, 52, 56–8, 78, 80, 104, 105, 113, 123, 126, 137, 138
Siraj-Blatchford, I., 25, 96
size, 9, 37, 72
Skinner, C. 101, 130, 146
social aspects of learning, 48, 64, 91
social class, 2, 46–7, 134, 135, 146
social interaction, 22, 33, 84, 94–6, 104, 106, 107, 124, 152
songs, 17, 26, 51, 53, 63, 85, 91, 100, 104, 150
    see also music
sorting, 26, 63, 143
spatial awareness, 58
speed, 4, 58
standards of achievement, 1, 3, 5, 44, 45, 136
    cultural differences in, 44
statutory schooling, 3, 18, 20, 44, 135
stories, 17, 26, 32, 34, 45, 63, 64, 67, 85, 89, 91, 94, 100, 103, 104, 105, 106, 116, 120–1, 149
structured apparatus, 69, 115
    see also resources

subitizing, 7, 8, 19, 55
subject knowledge, 41, 125–6
sums, 14, 49, 56, 66, 132
sustained, shared thinking, 25, 96, 97, 116, 132–3
symbolic language, 30
    see also hundred languages of children
symbol(s), 9, 12, 18, 30, 31, 54, 71, 72, 74, 75, 77, 102, 108, 109, 110

Tacon, R., 69, 115
teaching, 68, 83, 125, 138
    whole class, 94, 95
thinking, mathematical, 2, 3, 27, 28, 29, 31, 32, 69, 72, 82, 96, 98, 101, 109, 135, 137
    physical aspect of, 9, 145, 152
Thumpston, G., 30, 31, 50
time, 8, 9, 44, 48, 57, 58, 66, 113, 126, 143
    and space, 83, 85, 112, 113, 124, 135
Tizard, B., 3, 11, 44, 65, 135, 143
tools for thinking, 9, 71
transformation, 39
translation, 29, 30, 31, 48
Trevarthen, C., 8, 24, 26, 84, 118

visualization, 8, 86
vocabulary, 17, 70,80, 99
volume, 57, 99
Vygotsky, L., 47, 120, 136

Walkerdine, V, 47, 70, 73
weight, 14, 44, 53, 99
Williams, H., 69, 70, 71
Wood, D., 134, 136
worksheets, 19, 22, 49, 57, 63, 112, 114, 127, 128
Worthington, M., 11, 12, 17, 71, 72, 74, 75, 77, 89, 112–3, 114, 128, 130

Young-Loveridge, J. M., 135, 143